The Survival of
Small States

DAVID VITAL

The Survival
of Small States

Studies in
Small Power/Great Power
Conflict

London
OXFORD UNIVERSITY PRESS
NEW YORK TORONTO
1971

Oxford University Press, Ely House, London W. 1

GLASGOW NEW YORK TORONTO MELBOURNE WELLINGTON
CAPE TOWN SALISBURY IBADAN NAIROBI DAR ES SALAAM
LUSAKA ADDIS ABABA BOMBAY CALCUTTA MADRAS KARACHI
LAHORE DACCA KUALA LUMPUR SINGAPORE HONG KONG TOKYO

ISBN 0 19 215345 5

Printed in Great Britain by
Richard Clay (The Chaucer Press), Ltd.,
Bungay, Suffolk

PREFACE

There is more than one legitimate way of looking at political phenomena. Very broadly, they can be looked at statically, with an eye to structure, attributes, taxonomy; and they can be looked at dynamically, with an eye to function, relation, ecology. Neither approach can provide more than a partial analysis and a limited number of answers to the questions that are really worth asking; and the key test of the validity of each approach is the contribution it can make to the perfecting of the other. Yet no discussion can be conducted in terms of both approaches simultaneously. The difference between the two is dimensional.

It is for this reason that no apology is offered for taking up the subject of the politically autonomous small power for a second time. The first essay[1] was conceived essentially along the lines of the first approach—a static look at the subject. This essay is conceived in terms of its dynamics. In one sense it is narrower in scope because it is built around a deliberately restricted political topic: the small power in conflict with the great. But in other respects, so it is hoped, it is broader by reason of its direct political implications for a substantial segment of the contemporary international system.

It must also be said that this present book was a fairly long time in gestation and, perhaps as a consequence, my view of the methodology which is appropriate to a topic of this kind has changed somewhat since the publication of the first essay. The analytical scheme has been amplified and, as I hope, made more rigorous. It is now built much more explicitly around the notion of the paradigm. This has led in turn to the decision to construct the book as a whole on a base of case histories—in effect, the paradigms—each of which is discussed in detail, sometimes very great detail. In this way an attempt is made to illustrate and substantiate the general argument and to go some distance towards overcoming one common weakness of formal studies in international relations: the proliferation of general ideas without sufficient basis in historical fact and/or an excess of historical fact devoid of general ideas.

Some of the ideas and parts of the case histories which have been

[1] *The Inequality of States*, Clarendon Press, Oxford, 1967.

assimilated into the book have appeared elsewhere in rather different and abridged form. A preliminary and shortened version of the discussion on Czechoslovakia was published in the *Journal of Contemporary History*, vol. 1, no. 4. The analysis of the Arab–Israel conflict in the first part of Chapter Three is reprinted (with changes) from Spiegel and Waltz, *Conflict in World Politics*, by permission. Copyright © by Winthrop Publishers, Inc. The essentials of the general argument developed in the first chapter and concluded in the final chapter were presented as a paper read at the Seventeenth Nobel Symposium at Oslo in September 1970. I am grateful for the opportunity to expand this material and bring it together.

July 1971

CONTENTS

CHAPTER ONE

The Small Power in Conflict

Military force is not everything in the relations between states, but where there is both the capacity and the will to employ it, it necessarily overshadows all else. The mere possibility of its being employed suffices to transform the perspective of the policy-makers and to alter the anticipated material value—the 'pay-off'—of all other factors relevant to the conflict. The implications of its actual employment need no elaboration. Sun Tzu's dictum that 'war is a matter of vital importance to the State; the province of life or death; the road to survival or ruin'[1] remains eternally valid, even though the faintly romantic undertones carried by his kind of treatment of the subject may mildly appal us. It is undoubtedly true that force can, on occasion, be nullified by guile and dissolved by goodwill—and that is a source of comfort. But guile—or, more politely, political and military skill—is far from being the exclusive attribute of the weak, any more than goodwill is of the strong.

It is equally true that relations between states can be relations between the satisfied, such that the incidence and significance of military force in their common affairs is literally nil. But not all states are satisfied, nor all political leaders prudent, modest, and unafraid. Even if we were to believe, against all the evidence, that slowly and inexorably reason, restraint, sobriety, and generosity are in process of replacing fear, hatred, and ambition in high places and coming increasingly to determine the intellectual and moral climate in which matters of international policy are perceived and decided, it would still suffice for a single maverick member of the community to violate accepted norms for all the ancient and justly condemned uses of violence in the interest of policy to be re-invoked and re-employed.

Moreover, it is part of the common wisdom of our times that the anticipated terrors of general war between the major members of the international system are now so great and so well understood that no readily conceivable cause or quarrel could engender, let alone justify,

[1] *The Art of War*, translated by Samuel B. Griffith, Clarendon Press, Oxford, 1963, p. 63.

a calculated decision by any one of them to employ force in a conflict in which they or their firm allies are likely to clash with one another. This undoubted fact of contemporary political life has come, with time, to be something of an axis around which all other affairs revolve. It is one of the very few certainties, or near-certainties, of the system and it impinges in the clearest possible way on the structure and evolution of all international conflicts in which one of the great states which have equipped themselves with nuclear arsenals is involved—and *a fortiori* a conflict in which two or more such states have enmeshed themselves. Yet since Hiroshima there has been no drop in the *general* incidence of war—nor of political conflict hinge-ing on the possibility of war. It is only the possibility of warfare between Hiroshima's direct legatees—the great powers—and their truly close associates that has so remarkably declined. For lesser states the changes that have occurred in the structure of international relations since 1945 are hardly as dramatic. While the balance of terror constrains the possessors of nuclear weapons to be wary of each other its implications for all other states are increasingly un-certain. On the one hand, the continual elaboration of the modes of indirect conflict between the nuclear powers has heightened the exposure of unaligned non-nuclear powers to the direct employment of force against them. On the other hand, changes in the strategic needs of the nuclear powers themselves are making the grant of full protection even to aligned non-nuclear powers both less useful and more risky than it appeared to be a generation ago. The total member-ship of the class of states which are at present reasonably well shielded from the application of force against them is therefore likely to fall. Nor is this fall likely to be offset by anything approaching an equivalent rise in the number of nuclear states, for one other near-certainty of the contemporary international system is that those who are very powerful militarily have the economic and techno-logical capacity to become still more powerful, while the capacity of the less powerful to compete with them qualitatively, let alone quantitatively, is in decline.

The contemporary world of states is thus in the nature of a class society. There is, notably, a first class comprising those states which, by the very magnitude of their resources and capabilities and their consistent interest in the full range of international affairs, dominate the political scene and to a great extent determine the structure of the matrix within which the members of all other classes operate. They are also differentiated from the rest, perhaps more importantly, by the fact that while the rules of international politics which obtain today result, of course, from the sum of the activities and pressures of all states, these rules are not uniformly applicable to all states. And the difference is sharpest in the cardinal sphere of the employment of force as an instrument of policy. Basically, it means that force cannot be directly employed against members of the first class either by other members of that class or by members of different classes of states; force *can* be employed directly against the members of all other classes both by members of those classes and by members of the first class. Soviet troops can move into Hungary and join Egyptian forces in a declared war of attrition against Israel; United States troops can be landed in the Dominican Republic and their bombers can attack North Vietnam. The minor powers can certainly attempt to counter such moves on their own territory and on the territory of minor clients of the first class state with which they are also in conflict. What they cannot do is counter with an attack of their own. North Vietnam has not got the technical capability to bomb the continental United States; Israel may have the capability to bomb Odessa or Rostov-on-Don, but would never do so.

Up to a point, these have always been the implications of a strongly asymmetrical conflict. Since it is of supreme importance to the weak to avoid the application of superior force, they must refrain, if they can, from enlarging the scope of the conflict and raising the value of the stake—real or imagined—of the party which possesses superior force. But what occurred with the advent of nuclear weapons was a partial breakdown of the ancient mechanism which allows an imbalance between weak and strong to be redressed by powerful third parties. For today a first class power in conflict with a member of another class possesses not only vastly greater material capabilities— the capabilities on which its membership of the class is based—but also immunity to an entire range of military pressures and threats of pressure which, in earlier times, were employed at all levels of the international hierarchy. Other states cannot hope to acquire these capabilities nor can they hope to diminish the range of pressures to which they themselves can be subjected.

None of this is to suggest that the first-rate nuclear powers are totally immune to pressure, even certain narrow categories of military pressure, nor that minor states are—or need be—in any sense mere objects of policy, so much chaff on the winds blowing from Washington, Moscow, Peking, and in due course, no doubt, Tokyo. What is argued here is that given the intricacy and primacy of the connection between force and policy for all states, the central impact on the structure of contemporary international relations caused by the widening gap between the military capabilities of a very small number of states on the one hand and all other states on the other is not—as many suppose—to constrain the strong *vis-à-vis* the weak. On the contrary, it is slowly and inexorably to heighten the latter's vulnerability and narrow the political, no less than military, options open to them.

The problem this development sets the militarily inferior powers is, in a sense, the underlying theme of this book. But the word 'underlying' must be stressed. For to tackle the problem directly and comprehensively would be not only to grapple with too great a subject but also to lose whatever prospects of close argument and clear definition of the topic there might otherwise be. Instead, the book has been deliberately cast in the restricted terms of overt conflict between the small state and the great. This has been done partly for methodological reasons, as will be explained, and partly in the straightforward belief that the case of the small power which finds itself pitted against a very great one reflects, as does no other, the harsh aspects of present-day international politics that have been alluded to. No other set of circumstances evinces so sharply and dramatically the tension between a state's potential for action against opponents in the international arena and what, in actuality, its leaders have the energy, judgement, and skill to make of that potential. Moreover, as the class of first-rate powers is unlikely to grow significantly, while the membership of all other classes (and notably the class of powers that are without assured and recognized protection from members of the first class) will continue to rise, it would seem that the kind of problem discussed in these pages may now be losing its ostensibly somewhat unrepresentative, if not eccentric, character and that its significance for the future may well be much broader and its incidence higher than international relations at the time of writing might suggest.

(1) The complexity and infinite detail of international relations are such that it is possible to find evidence to substantiate almost any assertion one chooses to make. Equally, the choice of topic and data greatly influences, if it does not actually predetermine, the content of the assertions that are eventually put forward. It is therefore risky—and conceivably misleading—to embark on the discussion of any general question in the field without making the substance and rationale of one's method and the precise significance of one's major categories as clear and explicit as possible.

What is a 'small' power?

We tend to accept that some states matter more than others and unlike much conventional wisdom this almost intuitive belief is readily justified by any criterion one applies to distinguish what 'matters' from what does not. Only a small number of states can support the kind of electronic and metallurgical technology which has come to characterize our times. A still smaller number of states

THE SMALL POWER IN CONFLICT

support a culture and language that spills over and spins off on to other societies to a measurable and substantial degree. An even more limited number are today, or will be tomorrow, in a position to wreak world-wide destruction. And only a bare two or three can, if they choose, re-make the world order and bring back forms of imperial rule which have either faded from contemporary view or have been sufficiently attenuated to accord, more or less, with contemporary norms and needs. But the important thing is that whatever the standard or criterion, and however or wherever one chooses to draw the line between the Class A (or great or *primary*) states and the rest, it is easiest to do so in terms of an explicit or implicit definition of Class A itself. It may be a definition based on armaments, notably nuclear power; it may be a simple operational definition, such as 'that state which cannot be defeated in war by any other state or coalition of states without its exacting comparable costs from its opponents'; or the attempt may be made to formulate a somewhat more intricate operational definition, such as one based on the capacity of a state to assume lasting hegemonic leadership over others. Even a legal definition of sorts is available: permanent membership of the United Nations Security Council. And if this last definition is faulty and in part misleading, because the intentions of the formulators of the Charter can no longer be made to fit present-day realities, at least their intentions remain proper meat for the analyst's knife. At all events, it is clearly possible to define the Class A power in a broadly meaningful and useful, though not always wholly rigorous, way. In contrast, a definition of the 'middle' and 'small' power, the Class B and C state, or better still the *secondary* and *tertiary* power, is quite another matter, as a glance at the literature and, in particular, the published criticism of the literature, will show.[2]

The crux of the problem is to avoid two kinds of pitfall. The first arises out of the use of a definition which in substance is no more than the negation or transposition of the definition of the primary state—for example: 'members of the secondary and tertiary classes are those states which do *not* possess nuclear weapons'. For such a definition would merely be that of the class of all states less the great powers and would therefore come very close to a definition—or, more strictly, a partial description—of almost any state in the international context. We should then have to dispense altogether with the common-sense particularization of small powers, as distinct from middle powers (say, Malaysia as distinct from Indonesia, Ceylon from India, Uruguay from Brazil). Nor does one get around the

---

[2] See, for example, Robert O. Keohane, 'Lilliputians' Dilemmas: Small States in International Politics', *International Organization*, XXIV, 1969.

difficulty by transposition, which is to say, by setting an equivalent and parallel boundary at a lower level. It is true that at first sight a boundary drawn *within* the class of all non-primary states equivalent to the one drawn between the primary and the secondary (e.g. military potential or GNP) would, if it worked, provide us with the beginnings of a scale along which the position of any state could be rated and such that its salient characteristics could be inferred from its position. But in practice, the parallel boundary creates more difficulties than it solves and is apt to be illusory. It creates difficulties because it is impossible to correlate boundaries founded on any reasonably objective or neutral measurement (or indicator) with actual or potential varieties of political and military behaviour: the Gross National Product of Canada is approximately that of China, and the Swedish armed forces dispose of very nearly twice the trained military manpower of Britain. Such a boundary turns out to be illusory because it gives us no worthwhile political information and it fails to direct attention to what ought to be known; the complex reasons for Japan's 'low posture' in the international arena in the 1950s and 1960s are knowable, but they cannot be inferred either directly or indirectly from that country's economic, military, or technological potential, or from its internal political structure, or indeed any other indicator which lends itself to straightforward inter-country comparison. Japanese foreign policy has not only environmental and material bases, but historical, cultural, and socio-psychological roots which are by their very nature peculiar to Japan; or, if one prefers, characteristic of a class of states of which Japan is the only known member.

Some of these difficulties can be avoided by frankly taking common usage as one's guide and formulating an arbitrary definition which is based upon it. We know very well that policy-makers, no less than the general public, do tend to classify states semi-intuitively and to ascribe to them a loose and varying measure of 'size' or 'weight' or 'importance'. We also know that the place of any given state in the international hierarchy is unlikely to be stationary over a long period. Finally, we can see (if we look) that the classes prescribed by usage correspond to certain very broad patterns of behaviour—for example, the degree to which a given state will seek to influence affairs beyond its immediate environment and, more critically, the degree to which its leaders will be prepared to assume risks in the pursuit of extra-regional ends. It is therefore possible, on the strength of such admittedly unsystematic and probably unsystematizable distinctions, to point to groups of states so defined and seek to bring out the specific characteristics on which our view of them as a group or class ultimately rests. This is best done by detailed consideration of a member of the group which is so placed that those characteristics which interest us come clearly into play and into view. In practice, a state so placed will generally be, for that reason, an atypical member of its group; and not a model, but rather a paradigm.

The essence of such a paradigm is that unlike a model, it does not strictly purport to tell you how any member of its class will operate in particular circumstances. It tells you how a certain case, the paradigm, operates and wider uses then depend upon the extent to which examination of the paradigm throws light upon the likely behaviour of others. In practice, it does so best where it is a limiting case, that is to say where it indicates the limits beyond which the paradigm member of the stated class will tend to incur abnormal or counter-productive costs in the pursuit of a certain type of policy.[3] But if the limiting case makes for the most instructive paradigm, it leaves open the question of what might be termed average or median behaviour.

Thus paradigmatic analysis, for all its advantages, may incur the second pitfall into which attempts at a taxonomy of states tend to fall. The limiting case—say, North Vietnam just managing to face up to the United States and its South-east Asia allies—may very well serve to indicate how far a state of certain physical dimensions and resources can go and to suggest, by extrapolation and analogy, how and why others similarly placed might fare. But it soon becomes obvious that the limiting case is also the exceptional case; and from there it is a short step to the objection that by the standard of common usage which served as the original base-line it is not really a 'small' state at all, but a sort of dwarf great power, a political pocket battle-ship. On this kind of reasoning Czechoslovakia, which caved in before combined German, British, and French pressure in 1938 and again before Russian pressure thirty years later, all without a shot being fired, was a true and sufficiently typical 'small' power, *because* it caved in, but would not have been so had it resisted, least of all if it had resisted with some success (as, it will be argued, it could have done—at any rate in 1938).[4]

No doubt, the difficulty here is a common one that pervades the study of international relations as a whole. The varieties of condition and behaviour of states is very great and the number of subjects (states) very small. It is therefore extremely difficult to decide where to look for regularities and out of what material to construct the analytical schemata. But perhaps the more particular difficulty here is to determine in what precise relation the paradigm case stands to

[3] This is the procedure followed in the author's *The Inequality of States*, 1967.
[4] See below, Chapter Two.

the other members of the class to which it nominally belongs; or alternatively, whether the paradigm case, conceived as the exceptional state, ought not to belong to a very restricted class of its own.

All the approaches indicated, admittedly in summary fashion, rest on a *straightforward* correlation with the static, measurable human and material resources of the states, great as well as small, without giving proper weight to the evident distinction between permanent and intrinsic, as opposed to ephemeral and contingent, resources and advantages. However, if the matter is seen less in static than in dynamic and contextual terms, specifically in terms of the policy considerations of both the great powers and the small, which is to say, in terms of the characteristic issues and criteria which tend to arise, or to be employed, in the relations between the great and the small, then we can combine the advantages of the conventional, if imperfect, classifications of the great powers with those of paradigmatic analysis, but yet avoid the pitfalls referred to. We can do this by readily granting the primacy of the great powers and defining the secondary and tertiary powers in terms of the politics of the former, and particularly in terms of the balance of power between them. From this angle of vision the secondary and tertiary state's intrinsic and specific characteristics can be defined in terms of its relative value to the primary state as a political desideratum, or as a prize, or as a spoil—in a word, as an actual or potential *increment* to its total array of political and material resources. And seen in this light, it is immediately apparent that the nominally incongruous role of the dwarf or pocket major power—say, North Vietnam or Israel—is a *contingent* one, a function of unique circumstances, and subject to change in precisely the same sense that the relatively passive role of the great but quiescent state (say, contemporary Japan or Germany) is contingent, a function (in these latter cases) of special features of the post-1945 international system and clearly already in process of change. For the conflict between the United States and North Vietnam is not one in which (in American eyes) the central prize is North Vietnam, or even all Vietnam, any more than the prize in the conflict between the Soviet Union and Israel is Israel itself, just as the key question facing the Soviet Union is not Israel's international alignment. The political subjugation of either tertiary power by the primary power concerned, or its re-alignment, would not *in itself* constitute a decisive increment to either primary power's resources. Both, in themselves, are marginal and dispensable. In contrast, the present alignment of most of Germany and all of Japan with the United States is beyond doubt one of the central features of the post-1945 world; and losing either or both to the Soviet Union or

China would radically alter the distribution of actual and potential resources between the primary powers, perhaps irreversibly. Similarly, while the loss of Yugoslavia in 1948 was a bitter blow to the Russians, its long-term implications for the Russo-American balance of power were marginal; the loss of India by Britain *qua* primary power was fatal.

The operative importance of this distinction between the intrinsic and the contingent political and material capabilities of the state is that as the disparity of intrinsic capabilities between great and small powers grows, the capacity of the minor power to sustain conflict with a great power depends increasingly on contingent factors and on contingent advantages and capabilities; and, further, that the significance of the minor power itself within the general scheme of great power politics is essentially determined by its contingent role— its intrinsic capabilities being too limited to signify.

The small (or minor or tertiary) power, in other words, is that state which, in the long term, in itself and as a satellite or client or close ally—i.e. as a non-autonomous participant in international politics—can constitute no more than a dispensable and non-decisive increment to a primary state's total array of political and military resources, regardless of whatever short-term, contingent weight as an auxiliary (or obstacle) to the primary power it may have in certain circumstances. And it is its weight as a long-term increment to the major participants in the global balance of power that is the most instructive pointer to its finite resources—those on which will depend the outer limits of its action and its capacity to sustain conflict as its contingent advantages fall away. Among the questions that arise in this connection are therefore these: what is the nature of the contingent advantages which typically make it possible for a contemporary minor power to sustain conflict with a great one; and to what extent and in what circumstances are they likely to continue?

The small power that will serve best as the paradigm in terms of which these questions can be discussed, is one which is neither a 'pawn', in the sense that its policy is one predominantly determined by others for purposes extrinsic to it; nor a protégé or client or satellite, in the sense that it is not materially free to enter into definable relationships with more than one of the primary powers. It can only be the strategically isolated state, because unlike the 'pawn' it is an autonomous political entity and unlike the true client state its contingent attributes are subject to visible and rapid variation. From another angle of vision, the isolated state is one which is free to reverse such political ties as it may have when its intrinsic interests so dictate. The paradigm tertiary power is thus also one whose

B

behaviour patterns tend to be analogous to those of the primary power: it can neither avoid attempting consciously to restructure its international environment to its own advantage so far as it is able, nor rely for long on the support of others. But it obviously differs from the primary power in its ability to sustain the effort to induce change in the structure of international relations and such limited ability as it may possess is subject in turn to contingencies of which the key functional relationship is with the activities of the primary powers themselves.

The effective paradigm case is thus the acute case and the most acute circumstances for the tertiary state is actual or potential conflict with a primary state without the benefit of support from other primary states—because the latter may choose to be neutral, or because they are impotent, or because they are hostile.

(2) Three paradigm cases of conflict between tertiary and primary powers are discussed in detail on the following pages. The case of Czechoslovakia versus Germany (1938) is basically one of simple belligerent confrontation. The case of Israel versus the Soviet Union (in the aftermath of the 1967 Middle East war) is one of hostility mitigated in practice by balance within the intricacies of intercalated regional and global conflicts. The conflict between Finland and the Soviet Union is one which went through stages which were comparable in structure to the first and second cases, but which has now been largely attenuated into a *modus vivendi*.

Each of the three cases is intended to serve as an illustration of some of the themes out of which the analysis as a whole is compounded. But equally, each one represents an important stage in what is regarded as the probable evolutionary pattern of relations between the great (or primary) states and the rest of the world community, itself a most important component of the overall structure of international politics.

The case of Czechoslovakia is of enduring interest for a number of reasons. The fact that Czechoslovakia was able to sustain a war with Germany for a very considerable period points explicitly to what a minor state can achieve where it has the will to face a great and totally hostile enemy. It points implicitly to the great change in the terms of international conflict that has come with the introduction of nuclear weapons: no such direct conflict between tertiary and primary states could be envisaged today, let alone pursued. On another plane, Prague in 1938 is a study in the psychological pressures under which the leaders of a small and isolated state must operate and to which the lines of policy they adopt necessarily owe a great deal. On yet a third plane, Czechoslovakia may be seen as the prototype 'new state'—emerging insecurely from the ruins of an empire, only to be swept within a single generation into a second imperial system and then a third.

Israel's Middle East conflict with the Soviet Union is entirely contemporary in origins, in structure, and in the nature of the issues at stake. Its ultimate causes lie quite outside the narrow framework of specific Soviet–Israel relations: the major question *directly* at issue between the two states—the condition and aspirations of Russian Jewry—is fundamentally irrelevant to the conflict, and may be expected to be no more than very marginally influenced, if at all, by its outcome. It cannot be reduced, even for analytical purposes, to a 'duel' between unequal states; and, accordingly, the precise balance of military forces between the two has none of the operative significance that it had in the case of Czechoslovakia and Germany. The limits which the Soviet Union continues to set upon the intensity and scope of its material involvement in the conflict with Israel are quite easily traceable to elements of the complex which have nothing directly to do with Israel itself. In brief, to be understood at all, the Soviet–Israel conflict must be seen as a consequence of the intercalation of two separate struggles over logically and empirically distinct questions: the bitter struggle between Jews and Arabs over the existence of Israel, and the rather more gentlemanly fight between the United States and Russia for preponderance in the region as a whole. At the same time, it is the structural complexity of Middle East politics which moderates the conflict at its operational level, sparing Israel the punishment the Soviet Union might otherwise mete out to it. The really crucial questions thus concern the stability of this structure and the lines along which it may be expected to evolve. Part of the general thesis of this study is that the system as a whole is set upon a course leading to a gradual simplification of its terms—and the consequent loss of such contingent advantages as its minor members (i.e. Israel and the Arab states) now possess.

Finland is a state which lost the contingent advantages of balance within a complex primary power/tertiary power system, was duly forced to confront its great opponent in isolation, but yet escaped the fate of Czechoslovakia. It stands as a case of a small power which has managed to make its peace with a great one despite the issues which divide them, the accumulated effects of political and military conflict, and the price the minor member of the system must pay if the peace is to endure. As such, it points to an alternative, and somewhat more congenial, basis of relations than that which was initiated for Czechoslovakia after Munich and obtains to this day. The case of Finland represents neither a necessary outcome of the kind of conflict with which this study is concerned, nor a probable outcome. It

represents a possibility—to which, for reasons which will be out-
lined, closer attention should be paid.

Taken together, the three cases spell out many of the limits on the
ability of the minor power to operate independently in opposition to
very much greater international forces but they also reveal some of
the possibilities open to it. Each case may be seen as carrying either a
depressing or encouraging message, depending upon the observer's
own point of view. And each can serve, if only incidentally, to illustrate the simple truth that where the consequences of error are
catastrophic and the margin of error is extremely small, political
and intellectual talents of a very high order are needed if catastrophe
is to be avoided. The leaders of small states are rarely inferior in
personal qualities to those of great ones, although they are often
bemused by their lowly position in the accepted international hierarchy into thinking so. The failings and errors of the leaders of great
powers can be disguised and compensated for by the organizational
and material resources they can bring to bear. Even the awe in which
they tend to be held may suffice. But the errors of the leaders of
minor powers have immediate and unmistakable consequences and
are only too often beyond repair; and there is no disguising them.

In the final analysis, the condition of the small state which wishes
to retain its political identity and autonomy has elements of the
tragic. It may be sure of retaining identity and autonomy only so
long as its capacity for autonomous action is not put to serious test.
Conflict with a great power is, ultimately, a conflict over autonomy.
If it seeks and gains protection from another great power it loses
autonomy. If it remains unprotected, it is faced with unquestioned
preponderance of usable force which, because it is so clearly preponderant, the minor power can neither deter nor, *a fortiori*, hope to
overcome. The aim of the minor power must therefore be to avoid
such conflict; and yet, as each of the cases discussed here shows,
this is not always possible, and the effort to sustain conflict, with all
its uncertainties, may well be preferable to simple capitulation at the
outset. The heart of the matter is therefore the management of
conflict; but here too the minor power faces an irresolvable contra-
diction: it tends to be caught between incompatible imperatives—
between, on the one hand, the long-term need to diminish the
intensity of the conflict and, if possible, nullify its causes and, on the
other hand, the short-term, tactical need to raise the prospective
costs to the other side as high as possible.

CHAPTER TWO

Czechoslovakia—the Classic Paradigm

It is customary to consider the Munich crisis of September 1938 as, above all, a crisis in the relations between the great—or primary— powers of the day and as marking the last point in time when Hitlerite Germany might have been stopped by Britain and France. Much of the literature is, of course, polemical and it is a rare student of the period who has refrained from summing up his view of what the Western powers should or should not have done and what consequences flowed from the fact that France refused to honour its treaty obligations towards Czechoslovakia and was strongly en- couraged and abetted in so doing by the United Kingdom. It is somewhat rarer to consider German policy in an equally speculative light. The accepted problem has been that of ascertaining what German intentions were, or rather, when and how they were defined for operational purposes. The question as to whether any alternative policy could possibly have been compatible with the fundamental character of the Nazi regime has been faced only by a small band of revisionist historians. As for Czechoslovak policy, conceived as a choice between a number of possible options, that problem has hardly been considered at all. In other words, the assumptions underlying almost all analyses of 'Munich' are two: (*a*) German policy was fixed; (*b*) Czechoslovakia was an object of policy, not a subject, which is to say that not only was the Beneš government essentially passive in the event, but that it could not conceivably have been anything else. Once the primary powers had made up their minds and all Czech remonstrances had failed, there was, in their view, nothing left for the Czechoslovaks but to accept the ensuing *diktat*.

Ultimately, this approach owes a great deal—perhaps everything —to a deeply ingrained view of what the hierarchy of states entails for those powers which are both low in the international pecking order and unfortunate enough to be in conflict with states whose place is well above them. And it is the melancholy truth that the leaders of Czechoslovakia tended to accept this view of things, as did the leaders of the great powers.

The case of Czechoslovakia in 1938 is a study in isolation, in part self-inflicted isolation. It therefore remains the classic duel between great and small. What dates it in modern eyes is, perhaps, more than anything else, the fact that the modern primary power is vastly more powerful than were primary powers in the pre-nuclear age and that, in consequence, the modern tertiary state has—or ought to have— more to fear than its pre-1945 homologue. And yet what dates it no less is the fact that those relatively isolated states which find themselves in a position analogous to that of Czechoslovakia, which is to say in a position where they must face a hostile primary power without *assured* support from the latter's rivals, tend now to be less fearful and more self-reliant and to see somewhat more clearly that they must stand alone if they are to stand at all.

(1) In the years between the two world wars Czechoslovakia was commonly regarded as something of a model small state, a paragon of political sobriety and strength, certainly the most successful creation of Versailles. The Czechs were rightly held up to all as a living demonstration of what could be achieved in terms of economic welfare, international position, and substantial military power by dint of industry and application and a strong sense of national purpose. They received then the kind of applause reserved today for the Swedes, and for much the same reasons. There are two important differences, however. The population of Sweden is practically homogeneous, while of the fourteen or fifteen million Czechoslovaks in 1938 only eight million or so were Czechs. As for the rest, the Slovaks' attitude to the partnership was often quizzical, while the German, Magyar, and Polish minorities, amounting to a third of the population, looked at Prague with a jaundiced eye when they were not downright disloyal. The second difference lay in the fact that whereas Sweden is explicitly unaligned, Czechoslovakia was in formal, although in the event purely nominal, military alliance with France and, less directly, with the Soviet Union. Nevertheless, the problem of internal and external security presented by the minority populations could be seen as serving to heighten and spur the national consciousness and morale of the Czech possessors and beneficiaries of the Czechoslovak state. And the military alliances could hardly be supposed to constitute, in themselves, sources of weakness.

Czechoslovakia was then the thirteenth state in Europe in terms of area and ninth in terms of population; but it was seventh in terms of international trade. No less than forty per cent of its territory was of arable land and supported a rich and efficient agriculture. The country was endowed with great timber, coal, and iron resources. In

1937, 2,300,000 metric tons of steel were produced. The two Skoda armaments works at Brno and at Pilsen were among the greatest in the world; either was larger than the largest works of their kind in Italy. The illiteracy rate was extremely low, no more than four per cent, a figure which took in the backward regions of Slovakia and Ruthenia; for Bohemia alone it was 1·24 per cent. In 1930 over a third of the working population was engaged in industry and of these almost a fifth was in mining, metal industry, and the chemical industry. (No reliable figures are available for 1938, but the development of the economy suggests that these proportions rose.) Approximately ten per cent of the budget regularly went to education. The expenditure on defence was higher still: normally between fifteen and twenty per cent.[1]

Here then was demographic and economic potential of a high order, duly drawn upon to create a formidable military machine, as will be shown. Yet it failed to serve a concrete political purpose and played no role in the defence of the state when the test came in September 1938. On the contrary, much of it formed the nominal issue around which the 'Munich' crisis revolved and was surrendered under the terms of the Munich Agreement.[2]

The immediate military implications of Munich were, if anything, still more severe and striking. The Czechoslovaks were shorn of the better part of their fortifications and with them frontiers which, in most places, were on terrain that was advantageous to the defender. Again, the military advantage was never exploited, but formed the

[1] Figures for the years leading up to the crisis show the following:

Year	Total national budget (million Czechoslovak crowns)	Allocation for defence (million Czechoslovak crowns)
1934	8,880	1,327
1935	10,098	1,476
1936	12,433	2,276
1937	8,454	1,360
1938	10,117	2,098
1938 (extraordinary budget)		2,360

Figures derived chiefly from *Statistical Handbook of the Czechoslovak Republic*, 1943.

[2] Measured in numbers of employees, the Czechoslovaks surrendered—
29·6 per cent of their metallurgical and electrical industry
60·6 per cent of their textile industry
40·0 per cent of their chemical industry
30·8 per cent of their timber trade
59·4 per cent of their paper industry

Czechoslovakia in Maps and Statistics, 1944, pp. 38–9. Hubert Ripka, *Munich: Before and After*, 1939, pp. 231–3, gives other figures, higher ones, for the most part. Both sources are semi-official.

subject of the surrender. Against this gigantic blood-letting the consolation of getting rid of troublesome minorities hardly figured. In any case, three-quarters of a million Czechs were lost along with them.

It was a Carthaginian Peace without a war ever having been fought, or fought only in the minds of the Czech leaders, where they were defeated. For the Germans it was a brilliant victory.[3] For Britain and France it was—in the short run, at any rate—the successful outcome of a clearly defined policy. Daladier was less happy about Munich than Chamberlain, but the moving spirit in Paris, Georges Bonnet, was satisfied. The premises on which their policy was based may well have been faulty, but within the logic of their actions they were successful—firstly in compelling Czechoslovakia to pay the price the Germans required of them at the time, secondly in cancelling the substance, if not the letter, of the Franco-Czech Alliance. To persuade another to commit suicide where there is no inherent disposition on the candidate's part must be reckoned a considerable achievement.

Why the British and the French elected to do so, and how and why the Germans resolved to rid themselves of the 'spearhead' aimed at their side,[4] as they saw the Czechoslovak state, are questions that need not be entered into here. They have been dealt with exhaustively by a large company of historians and are, in an important respect, irrelevant to the present subject. The German, British, French, and Russian policies were all largely formulated before they impinged upon the Czechs. They originated in considerations and calculations that were mostly outside the Czech arena. When and in so far as they touched upon Czechoslovakia, the Czechs were at liberty to try to emend or alter these policies, but that is all. The Czechs could try to divert the great powers away from themselves. They could hardly hope to change their course. True, this *could* have happened, but speculation on this possibility is the province of observers[5] rather than of the statesmen actively concerned with the question at the time. In the event, the Czechs did not stand firm, but collapsed under the combined pressure of Germany, France, and Britain, particularly of the last two. They took stock of their position and conceded defeat.

It may be admitted at once that the only alternative for the Czechs was to go to war with the Germans—alone or in the company of others. Equally, it is idle to inquire whether the Germans were bluffing; for in the first place the bulk of the evidence shows that the

---

[3] 'To subdue the enemy without fighting is the acme of skill.' Sun Tzu, p. 77.
[4] *Documents on British Foreign Policy*, Third Series, (henceforth *DBFP*, the series number being omitted), ii, p. 347.
[5] It will be dealt with, briefly, below (p. 51 ff.).

Germans were preparing for war, both mentally and materially, and in the second place, empty bluff was not a possibility the Czechs— from their vantage point—could permit themselves to take into account. Thus, two questions—or groups of questions—arise, one chiefly political, the other chiefly military:

(*a*) How did the Czechoslovak government fall into the desperate situation in which it found itself in September 1938? Could it not extricate itself? And if it could, why did it not do so?

(*b*) What was the state of the Czech and German military forces with respect to one another? What was the Czech estimate of their relative strength? Did they act upon it? And if they did not, why not?

The military and political factors were all closely intertwined, and it is almost presumptuous to try to untangle them. This is particularly so because the military facts were often less important than the suppositions, estimates, assessments, and *idées fixes* with which generals and politicians alike were obsessed and which formed the heart of so many key—yet brief—conferences. But some attempt has to be made to compare the opposing forces objectively, if that is possible, in the light of what is now known, and then compare the result with what was then believed on either side to be the case.

(**2**) At the basis of Czechoslovak foreign policy lay the alliance with France and the cornerstone of that alliance was Czech military power. Masaryk and Beneš may have been, in their way, rather old-fashioned liberals, but they were not pacifists and they were, on the whole, unsentimental in their appreciations of world affairs. During the First World War they conceived and formed the Czechoslovak Legions to serve two ends: embody in the most tangible way the still unrecognized nationhood of their country and at the same time, by contributing to the general effort, lay a claim on the loyalty and recognition of the Allies. After the establishment of the Czechoslovak state much the same purposes underlay the very great effort put into the armaments industry and into the army itself. A small nation, they reasoned, surrounded by greater and lesser enemies, needs great friends. Tradition, political philosophy, the Versailles settlement, common interests, and sentiment all dictated that the alliance with France be made as secure as possible. The thirty-four Czech divisions—and more, if necessary—were conceived as a contribution that no French General Staff could ignore. Nor could Skoda and the other plants be ignored. Nor could the possibility of all this military wealth falling into the hands of the Germans be taken lightly; and President Beneš was prepared to remind French listeners of this factor 'dans l'hypothèse inconcevable de votre défaillance.'[6] Finally, there was Czechoslovakia's geographical situation, the spear in the side of Germany, or, as Hitler put it on another occasion, the 'aircraft carrier' in the heart of Europe. While active French interest in Czech military power evaporated with the general failure of French nerve in the face of resurgent Germany, this last advantage, the geographical one, attracted them to the end. (Facilities for French bomber squadrons were maintained in Czechoslovakia, whence Berlin could be bombed at a distance shorter than that between Paris and the German frontier at the nearest point.) This was important to the French, and Daladier was careful to explain its value to Chamberlain when the decision to attempt to impose a settlement on the Czechs was taken on 18 September.[7]

It is worth noting that there was never any question in anyone's mind of the Czechs refusing the French use of these facilities, nor, more generally, of their failing to join them in the event of a fresh Franco-German war. Certainly, in Czech eyes this was axiomatic as the price they had to pay for their security. The Germans twice offered them a non-aggression pact in an effort to draw them away from France—in 1933[8] and in 1936.[9] In the latter case, after the resounding failure of the French to respond adequately to the occupation of the Rhineland, there was an undeniable temptation to follow in the steps of Poland and accept the offer. On both occasions Beneš stood firm.

On the other hand, if it was the Czechs who were attacked, it was not seriously expected that the French would rush directly to their assistance. What was asked and expected of them was that they, in their own evident interests as much as in the Czechs', would declare war against Germany. On the military plane this alone would have the effect of automatically immobilizing a substantial part of the German army, and the Czechs, for their part, could limit their efforts to staving off the rest. On the political plane, the manifest intention of the French to stick to their undertakings would ensure the main object of the scheme, namely that the Germans would realize that war with Czechoslovakia implied general war.

It was a simple, brave theory, easily translated into an even

---

[6] Interview with Professor Henri Hauser on 10 May 1938. *L'Année politique française et étrangère*, xiv, 1939, p. 114.

[7] *DBFP*, ii, pp. 395–6. Daladier argued that in the view of the French General Staff the Czech Alliance presented considerable advantages to France. Though this was true enough he connected this with his demand that the British join in guaranteeing the emasculated Czechoslovakia. Chamberlain naturally could not see how this would be a substitute in terms of *French* security, but after consultation with his colleagues yielded, rather ungraciously.

[8] Letter from Beneš to Namier in L. B. Namier, *Europe in Decay*, 1950, p. 281.

[9] Edvard Beneš, *Memoirs*, 1954, pp. 14–20.

simpler national policy: everything must be subordinated to the interests of the French Alliance. In time Czech political loyalty to France became proverbial.

National purposes can—and, it may be thought, should—be simple. Their implementation in terms of policy can never be anything but complex. The temptation to seize upon the solution to the current problem, especially when it is well conceived, and project it into the foreseeable and unforeseeable future is entirely understandable, but it presupposes that the problem confronting the state remains unchanged. As this can never be, such a policy is almost certainly doomed to failure. In the case of very powerful states, particularly if their policy is aggressive, brutally simple national behaviour may attain its target over a considerable period. In the case of the weak state with less control and influence over the behaviour of other sovereign units, the period of the policy's success will be briefer and the onset of conflict of interests more rapid. If the policy of the small nation is specifically one of identification with a larger one for the furtherance of its own interests it may therefore be expected that sooner or later, as the mutual interests erode and as the views diverge, one of two results will follow. The small state will enter into conflict with the larger one; or else it will subside into vassalage, in other words be forced to subordinate its own interests to those of the master-state. It is true that in practice this very nearly ineluctable process may never be allowed to complete itself. Much depends on the tenacity of the parties, on the importance of the issue of the day and on the effective weight at the particular juncture of any of the thousand and one elements of an international situation. But nothing is easier than to set the process off.

For a civilized people like the Czechs there was the additional, special danger that a reasonably hard-headed foreign policy is soon converted—owing to its very simplicity—into a matter of principle, a doctrine. And, indeed, the French Alliance did ultimately acquire a certain sanctity. It was rude to question it. 'How dare you say such things of your country, you a Frenchman!?' said an indignant Beneš to his good friend Hubert Beuve-Méry, in the spring of 1938, when the latter came to warn him that he should not put absolute reliance in France.[10] The indignation was sincere. 'I know the history of France. She has never failed her word. She will not commence today', said Beneš.

[10] H. Beuve-Méry's testimony before the French Parliamentary Commission inquiring into the events leading up to the Second World War in Assemblée Nationale, *Rapport fait au nom de la Commission chargée d'enquêter sur les événements survenus en France de 1933 à 1945*, (henceforth *Les événements survenus en France*), Annexes (Dépositions), iii, p. 818.

The nub of the matter, however, was that the Czechs founded their belief in the permanence of their alliance with the West on the undoubted fact that both they and the French were beneficiaries of the Versailles settlement and its subsidiary parts. They were among the first to recognize that Hitler was intent on the destruction of the Versailles treaty and Beneš and his colleagues made the greatest possible effort, over a period of years, to convince all who cared to listen that the victorious powers and their clients must stick together. Hitler was bent on destroying the Versailles treaty, and the key to the Versailles arch was Czechoslovakia. It was therefore in the interests of the British and the French to help Czechoslovakia to help herself. By doing so they would enhance their own power and stave off a German *revanche*. It was a good case, sincerely held. It was persistently maintained to the end:

> Even if the Czechoslovak Government were resigned to the proposed sacrifices, the question of peace would in no way be settled . . . To paralyse Czechoslovakia would entail a profound political change for the whole of Central and South-east Europe. The balance of forces in Central Europe and in Europe in general would be upset; and this would not fail to produce important consequences in every other state and particularly also in France . . . Czechoslovakia has always remained faithful to treaties and has carried out engagements arising from them . . . She has been and always is ready to honour treaties in all circumstances . . .[11]

Thus the central argument of the initial Czechoslovak reply to the Anglo-French proposals of 19 September, rejecting the demand that the frontiers be redrawn on a basis of self-determination. Unfortunately, in reality the foundation of the case (and of the Alliance) had long since collapsed. The maintenance of Versailles was no longer the first priority of the French, still less of the British. The two governments were now concerned with one matter above all others: the avoidance of war. They held to this with great tenacity and determination, greater even than the determination of the Czechs to maintain their own sovereignty.

Habit, sentiment, and a prudish disinclination to question accepted political doctrine disguised the true state of affairs for a long time, at any rate from the principal participants. But of these it was the Czechs who were slowest to realize what had happened. Long after Chamberlain and Bonnet and even the reluctant Daladier had cleared their minds to the extent of understanding precisely what it was they now wanted, the Czechs were still labouring under the illusion that nothing fundamental had changed. An adjustment here and an adjustment there—and all would be well again. For a day or

[11] *DBFP*, ii, pp. 431–4.

two in the last week of September events almost seemed to justify this assumption. But this was a passing incident, almost a mistake.

The central purpose of the Czechoslovak government in the months leading from the Anschluss to the September crisis, and during September itself practically to the end, was to manoeuvre a return to the *status quo ante*. They hoped to do this by making a series of ever more substantial concessions to Western pressure. But here again the divergence in outlook between the two sides was revealed to all who cared to look. These concessions were demanded by the British and the French as steps towards the 'settlement' of the Sudeten German problem and as a means to appease *Germany*. The Czechs saw them exclusively as concessions to Western pressure in the interests of preserving their own relationship with the *West*. But in this the West had already lost much of its interest. Nevertheless the concessions themselves are important as stages towards the situation in which the Czechs saw themselves forced to capitulate. Some were overt and some covert and others appear to have been made with something less than due deliberation. But by 18 September, when the Anglo-French ministerial conference began in London and the crisis was unmistakably upon them, they had added up to a great deal.

On 23 July 1938, the Czechoslovak government had agreed to the arrival of Lord Runciman as 'Mediator'. On 4 September President Beneš had summoned the Sudeten Nazi leaders Kundt and Sebekowsky and accepted most of the demands that had been made in the name of the Sudeten Germans and embodied in the Carlsbad Programme (with a notable exception relating to Czechoslovak foreign policy). On 15 September Beneš had made a point of mentioning to the British minister in Prague, Newton, that at the Paris Peace Conference he, Beneš, had personally been in favour of excluding certain German-speaking areas from Czechoslovakia.[12] (This was duly reported to London, as it was certainly meant to be.) On the following day, the Prime Minister, Hodža, hinted to Newton that if some territorial cession was insisted upon it might be possible to surrender the areas Beneš had had in mind.[13] Finally, lest there be any mistake, the British military attaché, Lieutenant-Colonel Stronge, was on the day after (17 September) given to understand that the army would not object to such a transfer.[14] (This was very

[12] *DBFP*, ii, p. 333.
[13] *DBFP*, ii, p. 358. These areas were taken to be less than those which were ultimately covered by the Munich Agreement, but still substantial—with a population of between 800,000 and one million.
[14] *DBFP*, ii, pp. 364-5.

far from the strict truth, but the British could not know that.[15]) Thus by the time Chamberlain had returned from Berchtesgaden and was meeting the French ministers in London on 18 September, the assembled politicians and their advisers were all aware that step by step, under their own heavy pressure, the Czechs had made two vital concessions. They had accepted the Western powers as their interlocutors in their conflict with Germany, rather than the Germans themselves. They had accepted, too, that they must offer a territorial sacrifice. These were, of course, the two fundamental elements of the Munich Agreement.

The consequence of this steady retreat was that the participants in the London ministerial conference had no reason to contemplate too seriously the possibility that the Czechs refuse what Chamberlain believed he had agreed upon with Hitler at Berchtesgaden, namely that the solution to the problem they were presumably considering (the troubles of the German minority in Czechoslovakia) would be based on the principle of self-determination.

Daladier could be specific. He told Chamberlain privately, before the formal conference began, that he had received a confidential intimation from Prague that the Czechs would agree to concessions. 'So you see there is nothing we can do,' Chamberlain replied; 'Prague itself recognizes that.'[16]

In the course of these London discussions it was readily conceded that the Czechs would reject the idea of holding a plebiscite in the disputed areas for fear it would open the floodgates to demands from other neighbours. On the other hand, a straightforward cession of territory was a different matter. 'If friendly pressure were brought to bear on Prague, pointing out all the difficulties and stressing the necessity of giving up some portion of Sudeten territory,' then,

[15] Mr. George Ingr (letter to *The Times*, 8 September 1970) relates the following: 'Two weeks before the Munich Agreement was signed my grandfather, the late General of the Army Sergej Ingr KCB, as commander of the Central Army Group, met his other two army group commanders at his headquarters in Brno in order to discuss what the purely military viewpoint would be in the event of a Czech capitulation. The three generals decided that a capitulation would be sheer stupidity and it was agreed that Ingr should go to Prague as their representative and put such a position before the President, saying that the Army was completely against any surrender and would fight in any circumstances, no matter what the odds. Three days before the Munich Agreement was signed, Ingr arrived in Prague to deliver the ultimatum. On reaching the Presidential palace and stating his case, he was immediately arrested by Beneš and made "incommunicado" until the Agreement had been signed. He was then released, but it was too late: just as the international arrangements had been made, so had the blow to Czechoslovakia been struck.'

[16] Daladier related this to the French Parliamentary Commission. He was testifying under oath, after the war. There is no apparent reason to disbelieve him. *Les événements survenus en France*, Annexes (Dépositions), i, pp. 33–4.

Daladier felt, the Czechoslovak government might agree.[17] There remained only two points to discuss, since no one questioned Daladier's assessment of the Czech attitude. One was the necessity, in the French view, of guaranteeing the rump of Czechoslovakia, 'particularly in respect of the independence of their country during the coming weeks'. This was agreed to. The second point was the extent of the concession demanded of the Czechs. It was clearly going to be very much in excess of what the Czechs themselves had envisaged. This does not appear to have been discussed at all. Yet it was, together with the related issue of the modalities of the actual transfer, the subject of the subsequent clashes between all four parties to these negotiations—the Czechs, the Germans, the British, and the French. In any event, by the time the crisis opened with the presentation to the Czechs of the Anglo-French Proposals (to accept the Berchtesgaden formula with all its implications) the Czech position *vis-à-vis* the Western powers had been thoroughly eroded. As the crisis developed and as further *démarches*, manoeuvres, and concessions followed, it became increasingly difficult to reverse the direction of events and it would have required even greater courage on Beneš's part to embark on an ever greater clash with the West.

The Anglo-French Proposals of 19 September were a heavy blow for the Czechs because, if implemented, they would have meant very nearly as substantial an amputation of Czechoslovak territory, wealth, and military installations as later followed at Munich. True, the Czechs had resigned themselves to ceding some territory and hoped chiefly to limit the cession to a palatable minimum. When they now saw that they had miscalculated their first reaction was to temporize and to suggest a watering-down, specifically to return to what they themselves had already offered the Sudeten leaders and, at the same time, to invoke their Treaty of Arbitration with Germany. But the pressure that accompanied the Proposals was so intense that in very nearly the same breath the Czechs indicated that this was not their final answer.[18] Meanwhile they debated what to do—almost continuously from the early afternoon of 19 September to the afternoon of 21 September. Before them was the unmistakably uncompromising demand that they give a positive answer without delay. Chamberlain was due back at Godesberg for his second meeting with Hitler on 22 September and 'it might be disastrous if he should have to go without any answer from Prague'.[19]

The special horror of the trap they had prepared for themselves lay in the fact that there was now no significant difference, except in tempo of implementation, between what the Germans demanded

[17] *DBFP*, ii, pp. 389–90.   [18] *DBFP*, ii, p. 425.
[19] Halifax to Newton, *DBFP*, ii, p. 406.

and what the British and the French required; and even that difference was only to emerge clearly somewhat later. The alliance with
the West had been turned inside out and upside down. Instead of
easing the German pressure on Czechoslovakia, the British and the
French were adding to it. And because of the historical, ideological,
and doctrinal aura the Alliance bore in Czech eyes the Western
pressure was, if anything, more painful and more effective than the
German. In short, the Alliance had collapsed and the Czechs were
suddenly alone.

In these circumstances three courses of action were now open to
the Czechoslovak government:

(a) They could defy the great powers, rest on their arms, and await
developments in the full expectation of war with the Germans.
(b) They could appeal either to the Russians or to the League of
Nations or both and meanwhile proceed as above in 'a'.
(c) They could give in to Western pressure and seek to salvage what
remained of the traditional foreign policy and orientation.

To encourage the Czechs to adopt the third course the Western
powers had baited their demand with the offer of guarantees. Thus
the British minister in Prague could argue, quite plausibly, that from
the point of view of the future of the country it seemed to him 'that
the choice lay between worse than loss of everything acquired in
1918 and on the other hand the retention backed by a British
guarantee of nearly everything which they had gained in so far as
concerned the unity and independence of the Czechs and Slovaks
themselves and the territories in which they were a majority'.[20] This
was shrewd and concise. Beneš retorted that the guarantee he
already possessed had now proven valueless. Yet Newton felt he
could report his impression that 'President Beneš is more likely to
accept than to refuse and is very receptive to any reason which will
help him justify acceptance to his people.'[21]

It is characteristic that even at this early stage, namely the initial
presentation to Beneš of the Anglo-French Proposals at 2 p.m. on
19 September, Newton already had something more substantial to
go on than his 'impression' that the President would probably accept
them. The same morning (and therefore before the interview with
the President) the British military attaché had visited the General
Staff and had discovered that the substance of the proposals was
already known. He was also told that it was not proposed to resist
and that 'every officer . . . would obey the orders of the Chief of the
General Staff'.[22] It is almost inconceivable that this conversation

[20] *DBFP*, ii, p. 416.   [21] *DBFP*, ii, p. 417.   [22] *DBFP*, ii, p. 412.

should have taken place without authority, all the more so as it was anything but an accurate reflection of the true state of military opinion. One way or another there is thus every reason to suppose that the authority in question was the political one.

It is hard to escape the conclusion that the first two alternatives were never seriously considered by the government; and subsequent developments tend to bear this out. It may also be said that in view of Beneš's profound influence on events this is readily understandable.

By 1938 Edvard Beneš had been responsible for the foreign relations of his country for nineteen years, as President in the later years no less than as Foreign Minister in the earlier period. He was a most experienced diplomat and a professional statesman of the highest order. Hard-working, intelligent, educated, possessed of a first-hand knowledge of men and events almost unrivalled in his time, he was regarded not unnaturally as a consummate negotiator. In this he was strengthened by a gift that Wickham Steed—who knew him well—thought exceptional: 'Especially striking was his ability—an ability he shared with Masaryk—to put himself in the place of any foreign statesman with whom he might have to deal, and to think out his own problems in terms of that statesman's interests or prejudices. Thus he saved many a minister or politician in Allied countries from irksome mental effort.'[23] Such an ability has been an essential part of the equipment of the weak when dealing with the strong in all times; Wickham Steed was probably right in ascribing to it much of Beneš's success throughout the years. Yet this kind of sophistication can also be dangerous. It can lead to the placing of too great a stress on diplomacy and to a belief that by diplomatic techniques the statesman can do distinctly more than bridge minor gulfs and differences between states. There is a tendency in the successful diplomat—and Beneš was nothing if not that—to persist in believing that always, somehow, somewhere there is a solution waiting to be conjured up by a sufficiently gifted operator. This is perfectly natural; the alternative is for the diplomat, like a doctor at the deathbed, to retire and call in a representative of another profession. Loyalty, professional reflexes and a sense of responsibility are usually all too strong, however, for such retirement to be easy.

(3) Since the alternative to accepting the Anglo-French Proposals was war with Germany, something must now be said about the state of the German and Czech forces with respect to each other during

[23] Wickham Steed, 'Edward Beneš', in Jan Opočenský, (ed.), *Edward Beneš*, 1945.

C

this period, viz. in September 1938. The question of Soviet assistance will be considered separately; in any case it was conditional in the first instance on Czech resistance (over and above the problem arising out of the fact that the Russians' formal undertaking to aid the Czechs was conditional in turn on the French fulfilling *their* obligations).

The Czechoslovaks, as has been noted, regularly devoted between fifteen and twenty per cent of their annual state budget to defence. In the record year of 1938 planned expenditure rose to forty-four per cent. Whether these official figures fully reflect the costs of acquisition of aircraft from abroad, for example, is unclear. But they remain indicative of the effort made; and by 1938 there was a good deal to show for all that money.

The peace-time strength of the Czechoslovak army[24] was seventeen infantry divisions and four motorized divisions. However this could be rapidly expanded upon mobilization. When mobilization was decreed on 23 September 1938, some thirty-five divisions were formed; but even this did not represent the full strength available, as over and above the divisional formations there were some 60,000 special fortress troops, bringing the land forces up to the rough equivalent of forty divisions. Furthermore, the great September mobilization was itself not complete. A second line reserve equivalent to another ten divisions could have been called. However, as it is not clear whether there were sufficient arms for them, the total of forty divisions of land troops is taken as the broad measure of the effective strength immediately available.

Thus:

Land Forces:

1,250,000 men organized in fifteen army corps of thirty-four or thirty-five divisions; of these at least seven were of special troops, i.e. armoured, mountain, or cavalry formation; plus fortress troops.

[24] The figures that follow are all derived from published sources and represent an attempt to produce a collation by the usual methods of comparison. Though the details cannot be entirely accurate, the figures do suggest the orders of magnitude involved. It may be noted that no unreasonable discrepancies were noted in the information supplied by the principal sources which were: General Faucher, 'La Défense nationale tchécoslovaque, 1918–1938', in *L'Année politique française et étrangère*, xiv, 1939, pp. 85–102; Ripka, op. cit., pp. 134–5; S. Grant Duff, *Europe and the Czechs*, 1938, *passim*; Jiří Doležal and Jan Křen, *La Tchécoslovaquie en lutte*, Prague, 1961, p. 131; *The Times*, 27, 28 September 1938, and 24 March 1939; General Armengaud, *La Revue des Deux Mondes*, 15 April 1938, pp. 766–79; General Gamelin, *Servir*, Paris, 1946, ii, pp. 353–5; and *Czechoslovakia in Maps and Statistics*, op. cit. The League of Nations, *Armaments Year-Book*, Geneva, 1938, pp. 264–84, gives smaller, almost certainly outdated figures.

30,000 motor vehicles.
700 tanks.
16 armoured trains.
200,000 horses.
Over one million rifles.
60,000 light and heavy machine guns.
2,200 field guns (one source gives a figure of 3,200) of all calibres
ranging from light field pieces to 305 mm. howitzers.
2,500 anti-tank guns.
Air Forces:
60 wings equipped with 1,200 aircraft. Of these 600–700 were first-
line craft.

The principal deficiencies were in anti-aircraft and heavy artillery.

(The German forces will be dealt with below, but to put these
figures in immediate perspective it can be noted that the German
plan of attack on Czechoslovakia provided for the employment of
thirty-seven divisions organized in ten corps.)

The Czechoslovak army was a hardy, sober, and disciplined force.
It was well trained and its officers were well qualified for their tasks,
though some foreign observers had doubts about the professional
capacity of those generals who still survived from Legion days. Its
morale was high and the September mobilization demonstrated very
amply both the discipline and the loyalty of the reserves. Cases of
German or Magyar troops failing to answer the call or sabotaging it
were extremely rare. In any case, the great majority of the troops were
Czechs and Slovaks and the officer corps overwhelmingly so. Even
the non-commissioned officers were eighty-five per cent Czech or
Slovak. No unit had non-Czechoslovak troops in a proportion higher
than fifteen per cent and even then minority troops did not normally
serve in frontier areas.[25]

It was generally believed that the staff work was good. The
British military attaché in Prague reported on 3 September that the
Czechoslovak General Staff—'undoubtedly have a capacity for
organization, and I do not expect any serious hitch in the process of
rapid mobilisation, concentration or subsequent dispositions, except
in so far as these may be occasioned by enemy action. The whole
process has been the subject of careful study, and such lessons as can
be learnt from recent manoeuvres, the Sokols, etc., give ground for
confidence in this respect.'[26]

Their equipment was generally first-rate. It was produced for the

[25] *The Times*, 28 September 1938.
[26] *DBFP*, ii, p. 258. See also General Faucher's testimony, *Les événements
survenus en France*, Annexes (Dépositions), v, pp. 1191–1211.

most part in three large factories which were among the biggest and
most efficient in the world at that time. Besides weapons and vehicles,
the Czechs produced very good aero-engines. They were also
equipped with a plant for the production of poison gas.[27]

The essential military function of the Czech army was to defend
the national territory. In this task it was aided by the fact that the
pre-Munich frontiers ran through difficult terrain, except in the
south. To make the most of the natural advantages and to compensate
where there were none, the Czechs had constructed a formidable
chain of fortifications. At the outset of this work they had received
French advice and technical information. Later they seem to have
improved on the Maginot Line in many respects. It was an immense
complex of underground blockhouses and casemates, forts, electric
barriers, tank barriers, and underground aerodromes. By September
1938, all this was complete with the exception of the sector facing
Austria. Even there, however, the frontier was very far from being
easily passable.[28]

The German army at this time was by no stretch of the imagination
the large, self-confident, and victorious force that cut through
France and the Low Countries almost two years later. In April 1938,
its standing force was of no more than twenty-seven divisions, only
three of which were armoured, cavalry or mountain troops. It was
then estimated that by dint of special call-ups another eighteen
divisions of unequal value could be formed.[29] In the event, the
Germans did better. In September they planned to employ thirty-
seven active divisions on the Czechoslovak frontier, leaving five on
the Western front. Four reserve divisions were to back up the five
active ones in the west, together with fourteen Landwehr divisions.[30]
The latter did not amount to much. The three remaining active
divisions were left in East Prussia. Over and above this the Germans
were of course able to increase the size of the army after the fighting
had begun; the French estimated that they could do so at a rate of
fifteen divisions per month.[31] Nevertheless, as can be seen, the
thirty-seven divisions represented the maximum force available in
September for the attack on Czechoslovakia even on the assumption

[27] *The Times*, 24 March 1939.
[28] Robert Leurquin, a Belgian writer on military affairs, in *The Times*, 28 March
1938. Concerning the Austrian border, Henri Hauser asked Beneš whether,
through the Anschluss, Germany had not turned the Czech fortifications. Beneš
denied it and said that work on the Austrian border had begun before the
Anschluss. (H. Hauser, in *L'Année politique française et étrangère*, xiv, 1939.)
[29] Walter Goerlitz, *History of the German General Staff*, New York, 1953, p.
327.
[30] Telford Taylor, *Sword and Swastika*, New York, 1952, p. 210.
[31] Gamelin, *Servir*, ii, p. 347.

that no more than a covering force would be needed in the West or, for that matter, on the Polish border. The decision to risk leaving the Western front practically bare was a necessary and important element of the German plan.

The quality of the German formation commanders was almost certainly higher than that of their Czech opposite numbers, but the standard of the German troops was not. Many of them were still half-trained. Junior commanders and NCOs were deficient in number. The German equipment too was in many respects inferior to that of the Czechs, particularly the fighting vehicles and the heavy artillery.[32] Six months before, on entering into Austria, the new German armoured formations had disgraced themselves. Hitler later recounted how 'In the spring of 1938 we entered Austria. On the stretch from Linz to Vienna we saw eighty tanks immobilised by the side of the road—and yet what an easy road it was! Our men hadn't enough experience.'[33] On the other hand a higher proportion of the German army was mechanized, as indeed it had to be as it was the attacking force.

Thus in roughly measured terms of order of battle, quality of commanders and troops, morale and equipment neither side was obviously superior to the other. The Czechs had the benefit, however, of three strategic advantages, one of them immense. They were on the defensive without there being any question of more than limited tactical surprise. They had the advantage of interior lines. And, above all, they had their fortifications.

The Germans took the Czech fortifications very seriously and considered them the major obstacle with which they were faced. At a fairly late stage in the operational planning, Hitler had gone so far as to alter the plan of battle lest, among other reasons, there be a 'repetition of Verdun' and a 'bleeding to death for a task which cannot be accomplished' by von Rundstedt's Second Army. But it soon emerged that there was no way of avoiding the major fortifications entirely, for where they were weakest, opposite Austria, a 'thrust in the Fourteenth Army area will fail because of [lack of] means of transport'. Hitler therefore ruled that the motorized and armoured divisions should be assembled in the Tenth Army, which was based on Schwandorf and roughly opposite Pilsen, and that the major thrust be made there. Only then would the Twelfth Army, based on Passau and coming up from the south, strike through to the heart of Bohemia.[34] At the time Keitel denounced those who doubted

[32] *The Times*, 24 March 1939.
[33] *Hitler's Secret Conversations*, New York, 1961, p. 207.
[34] *Documents on German Foreign Policy*, Series D (henceforth *DGFP*, the series being omitted), ii, pp. 686–7.

the German ability to break through as planned. But at Nuremberg he admitted:

We were extremely glad that it had not come to a military operation because throughout the time of preparation we had always been of the opinion that our means of attack against the frontier fortifications of Czechoslovakia were inadequate. From a purely military point of view we were not strong enough to stage an attack which would involve the piercing of the frontier fortifications; we lacked the material for such an attack.[35]

As against this, the Germans could, *in the long run,* bring up vast forces to augment their effort. Taking the rough French estimate that a month after the commencement of hostilities the Germans could increase their forces at the rate of fifteen divisions per month, the German force could have been more than doubled by the end of the year, *provided there was no Western intervention.*[36] Clearly, if the military balance of forces is considered in total isolation from the general political scene and on the basis of a strict duel between the two states, there can be little question that Germany had it in its power to defeat Czechoslovakia. Where two states are of comparable technological and social development and where one population outnumbers the other five to one (or seven to one if the minorities are left out of the Czech account, as perhaps they should be) there is no apparent reason why the greater nation should not defeat the smaller if it has the will to do so. And of this last factor, the determination of Germany to impose its will, there was no question. What was in question was the time factor: the Germans were not convinced they would have a free hand for a sufficient period and it was therefore their clear purpose to avoid an extended campaign at all costs. It was on this issue precisely, whether Czechoslovakia could be speedily beaten, that Hitler and his generals were divided.

Hitler saw from the first that the attack on Czechoslovakia had to be conducted with the speed of lightning—*blitzartig schnell,* as he put it. This was foreseen at the now celebrated conference of 5 November 1937, and reiterated in all the operational directives. Thus, in the fully formulated 'Directive for Operation Green' of 30 May 1938, it was clearly stated that 'If concrete successes are not

[35] International Military Tribunal, *Proceedings,* ix, p. 2. (One of the difficulties was that the German 210 mm. howitzer was believed inadequate for the task of shattering the installations. Document presented to the IMT Nuremberg, quoted in Peter de Mendelssohn, *The Nuremberg Documents,* 1946, p. 77.)

[36] The British military attaché in Prague, commenting on a Czech General Staff estimate that 75 German divisions might be used against them, thought this two to one superiority 'not excessive in view of the defence and the interior lines'. Telegram dated 27 September, *DBFP,* ii, p. 567.

achieved in the first few days by land operations, a European crisis will certainly arise. Realisation of this ought to give commanders of all ranks an incentive to resolute and bold action.'[37] What the phrase 'a European crisis' was meant to imply was not noted down; but it was clearly intended to point to a catastrophe of epic proportions, conceivably one which did not bear thinking about in any detail.

The reasoning behind this insistence on speed is plain enough. Firstly, as has been seen, the Western front had to be left practically bare for lack of troops. Determination[38] and 2,000 anti-tank guns[39] were expected to prevent disaster if the French did move, but clearly the Bohemian campaign had to be completed and the bulk of the troops back along the Siegfried Line before Berlin could breathe freely. Secondly, the prospect of being bogged down in a long campaign in Czechoslovakia, even if the French did not intervene, went against Hitler's political grain. It was not merely a matter of prestige. It could have a disastrous effect on morale at home and drastically alter the picture Germany now presented to the West and to the Russians. It would invite intervention. It would change the political and psychological climate in which the Germans were operating. The time allowed for the completion of the task was, at first, 'a few days', later it was extended to eight. Whether viewed in its political or in its military aspect, speed was an essential element of the plan.

The Czechoslovak army, faithful to the political purpose and the strategic doctrine on which it was founded, was conceived by its commanders as a body that would act in strategic co-ordination with allied forces. A war in which Czechoslovakia would have to fight entirely alone had never been seriously envisaged. On the other hand, as has already been indicated, it was perfectly plain to all concerned that in terms of battle (as opposed to grand strategy), Czechoslovakia would indeed be alone and it was only *ultimately* that the full weight of Western military pressure would be turned against the Germans and the day saved. It was never for a moment in doubt at the Czech General Staff, or among other competent professional observers, that much of the weight of the German army would be thrown against them, but nor was there any doubt that they should and could withstand it.[40]

[37] *DGFP*, ii, p. 357.
[38] 'Ich sage ihnen Herr General die Stellung wird nicht drei Wochen sondern drei Jahre gehalten,' Hitler shouted when it was pointed out on 10 August that the forces would be insufficient. IMT *Documents*, xxviii, No. 1780-PS (Jodl's diary), entry for that date.
[39] *DGFP*, vii, p. 640. (It may be noted that this was something less than the Czechs had for their defence. See above, p. 27.)
[40] See Memorandum submitted to the Supreme Defence Council by the Chief

This salient feature of the situation was naturally seized upon by those who wished to bolster their desire to see Prague cave in politically with superficially realistic arguments pointing to the seeming hopelessness of the military alternative. Thus Geoffrey Dawson, editor of *The Times*: '. . . After all, with a great power like Germany surrounding your country on three sides, a row of fortresses in the hills cannot mean much more than the chance of holding up an invasion for a few days. It is a case of being killed on Friday instead of on Tuesday!'[41]

In practice, the immediate and crucial difference between the co-operation with the French they had originally planned for and what they would now be in for if their government decided for lone resistance was a twofold one: in military terms, the critical period would commence earlier, after, say, three months fighting, rather than six; in psychological terms they would labour under the heavy disadvantage of knowing they were alone in the ring with a powerful enemy and a group of hostile bystanders.

The Czech generals' essential confidence in their ability to withstand a German attack was matched by the senior German generals' dislike of Operation Green. Theirs was a technical and professional objection to the plan, not a political one. They did not believe the German army was ready for war, they had no confidence in their ability to charge through the Czech fortifications, they were fearful of leaving the Western front bare with a pitiful scattering of troops and a still incomplete Siegfried Line in the west, and they did not really believe that the feat could be performed in a week and the troops rushed back to the Rhine. In their view, too, there was a distinct danger of the situation degenerating into a world war. All in all, they believed they had a good professional case against Operation Green and they were unanimous and not infrequently outspoken in their opposition to it (Keitel excepted).[42] Keitel and Jodl inveighed against them, but it was indeed a good case and no professional grounds for ignoring it could be adduced. Jodl complained about

---

of the General Staff on 9 September, in J. Doležal, etc., op. cit., pp. 17–19. General Krejci complained of the tendency to underestimate Czech strength and overestimate the opposition. Also: views of British military attaché, *DBFP*, ii, pp. 258, 412, 567, 581; of General Gamelin, *Servir*, ii, pp. 353–5; of General Faucher both in the article cited and in his testimony before the French Parliamentary Commission; and almost all other authorities concerned. That it was also the considered view of the 2ème Bureau of the French General Staff may be gleaned from an article on the subject in *L'Europe nouvelle*, 24 September 1938.

[41] *History of The Times*, iv, 1952, 2, p. 935.

[42] B. H. Liddell Hart, *The Other Side of the Hill*, 1948, pp. 39–40. Also, Goerlitz, *History of the German General Staff*, pp. 328–9; and Taylor, *Sword and Swastika*, pp. 200–1.

their *Miesmacherei* and noted in his diary that the General Staff did not really believe in Hitler's genius.[43] This was very close to being the crux of the matter. Hitler had no military solution to the professional problem posed by his own requirements. He presumably hoped that it could be entirely skirted by skilful political moves; if not, what was lacking in plain military potential and capability would have to be made up with dash, daring, and inspired leadership in the field.

Two final points should be mentioned. Not only was the morale of the Czech forces high, but the Germans were convinced for a long time that the Czechs would put up heavy resistance. Not until 21 September, i.e. upon the acceptance of the Anglo-French Proposals, did the German assessment change.[44] However, two days later they had changed their minds once again and had noted 'the increase of the Czech will to fight'.[45]

Secondly, there appeared to be the possibility that a rising among the Sudeten Germans could be instigated upon the outbreak of hostilities, or even before. The Czechs were alert to such an event and the Germans, for their part, were actively so. A Freikorps was organized and armed Nazi formations were included in the German order of battle. A rising of sorts did take place on 12 September, but it was very firmly put down by the Czechs, thus showing what they could do when they had the will to do it.

It can thus be seen that it was the view of *both the Czech and the German military commanders* that the Czechoslovak army, unaided, could put up stiff resistance and keep the Germans at bay for a very considerable period, probably for several months, conceivably for many more.[46] Both the evidence available at the time and evidence which has since come to light supports this view. The defection of France did not materially alter this state of affairs. It was the political and psychological climate that had changed.

It follows that if the Czechs determined to resist the Anglo-French pressure and face the Germans alone it is at least possible that the Germans would not have succeeded in destroying the Czechoslovak state. The Czechs would have suffered a heavy hammering, but the 'European crisis' that Hitler feared would probably have occurred. True, the final outcome of such resistance could not be foretold with

[43] Jodl's diary, entry for 10 August 1938, in IMT *Documents*, No. 1780-PS.

[44] Jodl's diary for 22 September. See also E. M. Robertson, *Hitler's Pre-War Policy*, 1963, pp. 142-3.

[45] Jodl's diary for 23 September.

[46] There was a plan to retreat gradually to a redoubt in the eastern half of the country, and to that end arms factories had been established there. The French had encouraged the Czechs to do so.

any certainty. If it was certainty that was sought—it could only be found in surrender.[47]

(4) Precisely what occurred during the forty-eight hours or so of what must have been the heart-rending and humiliating debate in which the Czech authorities discussed the Anglo-French proposals has never been made public. Authoritative Czech spokesmen[48] have almost universally preferred to shift attention to the debate between the Czech authorities and the Western powers. This reticence is, in view of the circumstances, perfectly comprehensible and not in the least dishonourable; but makes it mandatory that any attempt to understand what transpired must rely on a fairly high degree of conjecture.

It must be remembered that the Anglo-French Proposals, severe and unpalatable though they were, did not specify a timetable for the transfer of territories to the Germans, nor did they go into the modalities of such a transfer. The transfer meant a great loss of wealth, military installations, and skilled and efficient citizens. It meant too that there would be a loss of strategically advantageous borders. A new, weakened Czechoslovakia was implicit in the cession, but though it was offensive to national pride and extremely disturbing to those responsible for the defence of the country, it was nevertheless just conceivable that the refashioned state would be viable.

[47] It may be idle to speculate how the campaign would have developed had it ever started. Yet it is interesting to recall that the original German plan for the invasion of France in 1940 was drawn up under Halder and was to be executed by very much the same group of senior commanders responsible for 'Green'. Like 'Green' it was a conservative plan. In Liddell Hart's view it was 'broadly similar to that of 1914 . . . It is clear now that if the plan had been carried out it would have failed to be decisive.' It was Manstein, a relatively junior commander, who saw its drawbacks and offered a more daring scheme. When his superiors rejected it he took it to Hitler and it was adopted. So far as the French were concerned, it was not, in Liddell Hart's view, the Maginot Line that failed them, but the offensive side of their plan. 'By pushing into Belgium with their left shoulder forward they played into the hands of their enemy, and wedged themselves into a trap.' (See B. H. Liddell Hart, *The Other Side of the Hill*, pp. 118–22.)

It might be added, parenthetically, that the Czech high command proposed to make the most of their fortifications against which, they hoped, the insufficiently trained German soldier would throw himself. It was expected that the first failures to take fortified positions would have a disastrous effect on German morale. (See Chief of Staff's Memorandum in J. Doležal and Kren, *La Tchécoslovaquie en lutte*.)

[48] Such as Hubert Ripka. Left-wing accounts (e.g. 'Pierre Buk', *La Tragédie tchécoslovaque*, Paris, 1939, and more recent accounts published in Prague after the war) tend to lay great stress on Agrarian Party machinations. In view of Beneš's immense authority it would seem that the net effect of such pressure could not have been decisive.

General Syrový was to say in his apologetic broadcast of 30 September:

> Our State will not be one of the smallest in the world. There are others which are much smaller, and yet they are sound and resistant. We shall have enough territory left to give us the possibility of further cultural and economic progress. It is true that we shall live within narrower boundaries, but we shall be entirely among ourselves. Many hindrances to the good and peaceful administration of our State will be removed. Agreement with our neighbours, too, will be easier. Our Army will continue to have its task and will protect the nation and the State and will continue to be on guard as formerly.[49]

If this was true after Munich, it was true *a fortiori* nine days before.

As far as national security was concerned, the loss of strategic frontiers could perhaps be offset by Britain joining France formally in guaranteeing Czech independence. It could be argued further, that as against the implied cancellation of the Franco-Czech Alliance there was an international, Anglo-French guarantee: a new relationship with the West, suited to the new times, deriving much of its force from the fact that it was to be proclaimed at this difficult moment. It was a hard thing to go to war over the difference between what had already been conceded and what was now demanded—and lose the life-line to the West in the bargain. All this could be argued. But in any case, as we have seen, the minds of those in authority were already largely made up by the morning of 19 September.[50]

There was another problem. It was clear to the President and to most of those who had actual dealings with the Western statesmen and diplomats that the Western powers would not hesitate to use any available weapon in the political armoury. They were intent on a Czechoslovak surrender and as they saw the issue as one of life and death to themselves no argument could be expected to sway them. At the same time, Czechoslovakia had not merely a moral, but a well-known formal and legal right to insist on their support against Germany. It was therefore not enough for the Czechoslovak *government* to sense, or even to know, that a renunciation of Western obligations towards Czechoslovakia was impending. The renunciation had to be clear and public too. If the Western powers—France in particular—baulked at this and fought shy of actually certifying their refusal to honour the obligation, so much the better. A considerable diplomatic battle would have been won. If, on the other hand, the West swallowed hard and went through with the betrayal, then at least the government in Prague would be spared the charge

---

[49] Royal Institute of International Affairs (RIIA), *Documents on International Affairs, 1938*, ii, p. 328.
[50] *DBFP*, ii, p. 412, already quoted.

of infirmity and of failing to explore all available avenues of escape. But the danger then was that the betrayal would be followed by abandonment and that in the event of a general European war the same coalition of great states would be ranged against Czechoslovakia in its aftermath, much as they now confronted it in its opening stages. In brief, having decided against resistance, the problem facing Prague was to save as much as possible from the wreckage. And the solution, in practice, was to keep up the stiffest possible resistance to the Anglo-French pressure at one level, while keeping the lines open to Paris and London at the other.

On 20 September, approximately twenty-four hours after his interview with Beneš, Newton telegraphed London that he had had it from a very good source [51] that the official reply just handed him that evening 'should not be regarded as final'. He went on,

A solution must however be imposed upon the Government as without such pressure many of its members are too committed to be able to accept what they realize to be necessary.

If I can deliver a kind of ultimatum to President Beneš, Wednesday, he and his Government will feel able to bow to *force majeure*. It might be to the effect that in the view of His Majesty's Government the Czechoslovak Government must accept the proposals without reserve and without further delay failing which His Majesty's Government will take no further interest in the fate of the country.

I understand that my French colleague is telegraphing to Paris in a similar sense. [52]

Lacroix, the French minister did indeed send a telegram, one which was later the subject of much dispute since part of it was exploited by the French Foreign Minister in the public debate that followed Munich. [53] After the war, Lacroix told the French Parliamentary Commission of Enquiry what had occurred:

... M. Hodža, Président du Conseil, me convoqua par téléphone. J'interrompis aussitôt mon travail pour me rendre à son invitation. M. Hodža me demanda si j'étais certain que la France se déroberait en cas de conflit. Je lui répondis que je n'en savais rien et je lui proposai de télégraphier immédiatement à Paris pour avoir une réponse ferme. Il m'objecta que cette démarche serait trop longue et ajouta: 'J'admets *a priori* que la France ne marchera pas et si vous pouvez cette nuit même obtenir de

[51] Hodža?

[52] *DBFP*, ii, p. 425.

[53] See H. Beuve-Méry, 'La vérité sur la pression franco-britannique' in *L'Europe nouvelle*, 29 October 1939; and J. W. Wheeler-Bennett, *Munich*, 1948, p. 122. Georges Bonnet, Hubert Beuve-Méry and Lacroix himself were all closely questioned on the subject when they testified before the Commission. Lacroix's evidence is convincing.

votre gouvernement un télégramme le confirmant, le Président de la
République s'inclinera. C'est le seul moyen de sauver la paix.[54]

Lacroix duly received his telegram certifying the French decision
to disassociate themselves from Czechoslovakia's fate and Newton
got his ultimatum. The celebrated audience with Beneš at just past
two o'clock in the morning of 21 September ensued.[55]

It was a long and painful interview. Beneš pointed out his detailed
objections to the plan and asked for clarification of a number of
points, including the precise nature of the guarantee offered. Then
he justified his country's foreign policy and stated that in pursuing
it 'he had not been driven by the Soviet government which he had
kept to one side'. He warned that internal troubles must be expected
and did not know whether the government could control them.
Finally, towards the end:

> M. Beneš said that he took our *démarche* to be a kind of ultimatum and
> indeed only such an ultimatum could justify him and his Government in
> accepting the Anglo-French proposals without obtaining beforehand the
> sanction of Parliament as was constitutionally required. We therefore told
> him that our *démarche* had the character of an ultimatum in the sense that
> it represented the final advice of our Governments and in their view the
> last possible moment for acceptance of their advice, if this country was to
> be saved.[56]

By carefully pointing out to the Western representatives that he
had not been guided by the Russians, Beneš left them free to understand that Czech policy would remain dissociated from the Soviet
Union's. Later, it was often argued on his behalf that one of the main
considerations underlying his policy was fear of a situation where his
country would find itself fighting with the Russians against the
Germans, with the West on the sidelines or, worse, participating in a
general crusade against communism. It is not clear how real this fear

[54] *Les événements survenus en France*, Rapport, ii, p. 268. The question has been
raised whether Hodža had Beneš's authority for his request or not. Lacroix, at
any rate, did not doubt it at the time. Nevertheless, he told the Commission that
Beneš's capitulation, in itself, surprised him. Even in retrospect he could not
quite understand it and thought that internal difficulties, i.e. Agrarian Party
pressure, might have been a cause. For, said Lacroix, 'à première vue . . . le
Président Beneš n'avait aucune raison de capituler puisque l'armée était prête à
entrer en guerre et que le Parlement était en vacance. Je me suis toujours
demandé si le courage ne lui à pas manqué au dernier moment.'

[55] Halifax's telegram to Newton (*DBFP*, ii, p. 437) did not specifically refer to
the telegram cited here. But as Newton's message was received in London at
10.45 p.m. and Halifax's message was dispatched at 1.20 a.m., it can be safely
assumed to have reached the Foreign Secretary in time.

[56] *DBFP*, ii, p. 450.

was. But what assuredly did weigh heavily with him was his undoubted conviction that a national revival, such as the Czechs', must
be inextricably joined to political democracy. Without nationalism
democracy had no future in Central Europe; without democracy
nationalism all too rapidly degenerated into fascism. Unaided and
unsupported by the Western democracies, Czechoslovak liberalism
could not long survive an alliance with the Soviet Union.

Nevertheless, the Czechs were careful to maintain friendly con-
tact with the Russians and explore the possibilities of assistance,
should it be decided to call for their aid; and when the crisis came
the Russians were duly informed. On 19 September Beneš summoned the Soviet minister, Alexandrovsky, and informed him of the
Anglo-French Proposals and what was implied thereby. He also told
the minister that the government had rejected the proposals. Beneš
then put two questions to the Russian. Would the Russians fulfil
their undertakings if France did too? And, as Czechoslovakia would
appeal to the League in the event of an attack, would the Soviet
Union render assistance as a member of the League under Articles
16 and 17? [57]

The Beneš who emerges from the Soviet diplomat's dispatch is
tougher and more critical of the West than the one delineated in the
reports of the Western envoys. But in any event, the Russians lost no
time in giving Beneš an affirmative and unequivocal answer to both
his questions. [58] They also informed the French of the answer they
were transmitting to the Czechs. This was on 20 September, before
the final confrontation with the Western representatives. On 21
September Litvinov told the Assembly of the League of Nations
about the Czech query and of the Soviet answer, and also about a
French query in the same vein that had preceded it. [59] Thus, having
backed their privately transmitted replies with a public statement,
the Russians' position was rendered formally impeccable. They appear to have wondered why the Czechs did not ask them outright
whether they would offer *unconditional* aid if so requested, but did
not insist [60]—possibly because a request for, or an offer of, unilateral
military aid, i.e. one which had neither the cover of a League of
Nations resolution nor the co-operation of the Western powers,
would necessarily have implied invasion of Rumania or Poland under
the worst possible circumstances and they were clearly reluctant to
enter into a conflict with Germany with the strong possibility that

[57] *New Documents on the History of Munich*, Prague, 1958, pp. 86–8 (henceforth, *New Documents*).
[58] Ibid., p. 90.
[59] RIIA, *Documents on International Affairs, 1938*, ii, pp. 224–5.
[60] *New Documents*, p. 109.

much of Europe would be arrayed against them.[61] But to be set against the Soviet reluctance to enter into such a conflict was the Czechoslovak reluctance to invite them to do so.

All of this was, however, subsidiary to the main business of the relations with the Western powers. The circular telegram of 21 September from the Foreign Minister, Krofta, to Czech Missions abroad reviewing developments did not mention it and concluded, simply, with the following paragraph: 'In view of this [Anglo-French] ultimatum, and being completely isolated, the Czechoslovak Government will evidently have to yield to irresistible pressure. An answer will be handed to the British and French Ministers in the course of to-day.'[62]

(5) On the day after the Czech surrender to the Anglo-French pressure the Sudeten German *Freikorps* entered Czech territory and occupied the border towns of Asch and Eger. 'Reichgerman' SA and SS units joined them. Meanwhile the German army proper continued to move towards the frontier in accordance with the Operation 'Green' timetable, and a fully orchestrated and typically vicious propaganda campaign was loosed against Czechoslovakia. When, on the same day, Chamberlain met Hitler at Godesberg—with the Czech capitulation in his pocket—he was met with new demands. Briefly put, these were that the 'German' territories of Czechoslovakia—to be delineated by the Germans themselves—were to be transferred to German authority within eight days. After the occupation by German troops a plebiscite could be held in those areas; a plebiscite would in any case be held in other areas not immediately occupied. What all this meant, in plain terms, was that a panic flight of Czechs, Jews, German Social-Democrats, and other potential victims of the Germans would ensue, that the Czech forces would not have time to remove their stores, nor destroy their installations, nor organize new defences before evacuation, and that, to crown it all, the entire procedure would be deliberately and unmistakably humiliating. As the Czechs rightly pointed out, the Godesberg Memorandum was 'a *de facto* ultimatum of the sort usually presented to a vanquished nation and not a proposition to a sovereign state'.[63] Chamberlain was appalled and angered and, after concluding that Hitler could not be shaken, returned to London. Moreover, before leaving Germany, he had reluctantly agreed with Halifax that in view of the German troop movements 'the French and British

[61] Cf. Fierlinger's dispatch of 17 September quoted in William V. Wallace, 'New Documents on the History of Munich', *International Affairs*, October 1959, p. 453.
[62] *New Documents*, p. 100.   [63] *DBFP*, ii, p. 519.

Governments cannot continue to take responsibility of advising them not to mobilize'.[64] The Czechs, who until then had obeyed the injunction not to mobilize,[65] promptly and joyfully did so. In the event, the mobilization was an immense organizational success and provided convincing proof of the high state of national morale and of the popular feeling against a capitulation. 'No one who was there to see,' reported the special correspondent of *The Times*, 'could ever forget the quietness and dignity with which the Czechoslovak nation took up their arms on Friday night.'[66]

Thus by the time the Czech government met to consider the Godesberg terms on 25 September[67] the situation seemed to have changed significantly. At home, reconstituted under General Syrový, they were riding on a new crest of popularity. Abroad, they could well believe that the Germans had finally and irrevocably revealed how brutal, unscrupulous, and insatiably ambitious they were and that it was in the light of general recognition of the true state of affairs that the French and British ministers were meeting in London. Even the Czechs themselves had very properly been asked to send a delegation and make plain their views. The nightmare of isolation appeared to be over and the policy of acceding to Western wishes in order to retain Western friendship seemed to have justified itself. War was probably inevitable,[68] but no blame could be attached to them for Czechoslovakia had done all in its power to save the peace. It was urgently necessary to secure Polish neutrality in the event of war,[69] but for the rest Prague could await developments. Thus fortified, the Czechs felt they could reject the German terms and face the prospect of war with all the necessary courage and with a determination eloquently expressed in Jan Masaryk's formal Note to Halifax: '. . . My Government wish me to declare in all solemnity that Herr Hitler's demands in their present form are absolutely and unconditionally unacceptable to my Government. Against these new and cruel demands my Government feel bound to make their utmost resistance and we shall do so, God helping. The nation of St.

[64] *DBFP*, ii, p. 461. The instructions to communicate the message were given separately (ibid., p. 485) by the Prime Minister and (ibid., p. 483) by Halifax.

[65] See for example, *DBFP*, ii, p. 491.

[66] *The Times*, 26 September 1938. See also A. Henderson, *Eyewitness in Czechoslovakia*, 1939, p. 217; and Colonel Stronge's indignant comment on doubts cast by his colleague at *Berlin* on the morale of the Czech Armed Forces, *DBFP*, ii, pp. 581–2. There is abundant evidence to support his views in all the sources, Czech, French, British, and German.

[67] They did not receive the full text until the night of 24/25 September.

[68] Letter from Beneš to L. B. Namier, 20 April 1944, quoted in L. B. Namier, *Europe in Decay*, p. 281.

[69] Idem.

Wenceslas, John Hus and Thomas Masaryk will not be a nation of slaves.' And then, following immediately, the last paragraph of the Note: 'We rely upon the two great Western democracies, whose wishes we have followed much against our own judgment to stand by us in our hour of trial.'[70]

However, the illusion that the Western powers would now support them was of brief duration. The intense fear and detestation of war that had motivated the dominant members of the British and French governments was not in the least diminished by the general feeling that war might really be imminent. After a little while, when the immediate shock of Godesberg had lapsed, the British pulled themselves together and dispatched Sir Horace Wilson to Hitler—on the grounds that '. . . so long as there remained even a slender chance of peace, we must not neglect any opportunity of securing it'.[71] Characteristically, this was done before the Anglo-French ministerial conference had ended or had even arrived at any considered judgement on the policy to adopt. What the *Czechs* thought now mattered less and less and from this point on they ceased to address themselves seriously to the government in Prague. Newton's instructions, in essence, were merely to calm their growing fears: 'You should explain to the Czechoslovak Government that the communication which is being made to the German Chancellor through Sir Horace Wilson in no way prejudices the position of the Czechoslovak Government.'[72]

There can be little doubt that the profound fear and hatred of war which swept over London and Paris once more was the major source of Czechoslovak weakness *vis-à-vis* the Western powers. But there was a second, only marginally less considerable one: the concessions the Czechs had already made and which continued to dog them. For by this stage, if looked at in a sufficiently cold-blooded manner, the difference between what they had already agreed to (i.e. the Anglo-French Proposals), and did not even now denounce, and what the Germans nominally required of them, could be made to appear technical and procedural. It concerned not the principle of cession, but 'the way in which the territory is to be handed over'.[73] And this, in Chamberlain's view, could (and therefore should) be settled by agreement. No doubt, as he knew and stated in his letter to Hitler (quoting Masaryk), the Germans were demanding a procedure that was harsh in the extreme, and which put Czechoslovak national security at risk. But it was nevertheless an incremental difference, a

[70] *DBFP*, ii, p. 519.
[71] Chamberlain to the assembled ministers, 26 September, in *DBFP*, ii, p. 537.
[72] *DBFP*, ii, p. 544.
[73] From Chamberlain's letter to Hitler, 26 September, *DBFP*, ii, p. 542.

D

marginal addition to the great concession that had already been made. It was easy enough for the outsider to seize upon this fact (as Chamberlain did) but, on the other hand, it required considerable gifts of empathy (which he lacked) to put it in its proper perspective.

The battle for the minds of the Western leaders was one the Czechs were bound to lose and the Germans to win. The former could only point to the injustice and the cruelty that would be done them. The latter could (and did) argue that the Czechs were viciously intent on precipitating a general war to avoid fulfilling their undertakings to hand over the Sudeten territories.[74] In these circumstances, the best German tactic was to stand firm. And this, despite their nervousness, the mutterings of the generals, and—in many cases—their own unwillingness to go to war at this time, they did. Doubtless, Hitler's iron nerve held them together. At any rate, the debate was now conducted on this basis and it is hard to see how it could have had any other issue but a demand that the Czechs make one last, marginal concession.

At the Four Power conference at Munich that followed on 29 September, the question whether the Czechoslovaks would accept the emerging *diktat* hardly arose seriously. When it was mentioned it was promptly dismissed by Hitler on the grounds that if they rejected it they would prove they only respected force.[75] Towards the end the conferees did ask themselves, what is to be done about the Czechs? But their concern was only with the technical question of how the terms of the Agreement were to be transmitted to them. The actual demand to accept the terms, when it came, was unashamedly peremptory. 'You will appreciate that there is no time for argument,' Chamberlain telegraphed Newton from Munich; 'it must be plain acceptance.'[76]

(6) By the time the Four Power Agreement, which encapsulated the combined assault of Germany, Britain, and France (and Italy) upon them, was in the hands of the Czechs (at 6.15 on the morning of 30 September) the other, Polish assault had reached fruition.

---

[74] As for example, in Hitler's talk with Sir Horace Wilson, 27 September, *DBFP*, ii, pp. 564–7.

[75] At one point Chamberlain remarked soberly that he could not guarantee complete evacuation by the Czechs without destruction of installations because, among other reasons, the Czechs had not yet accepted the terms of the Agreement. At this Hitler got very excited and after some argument the matter was dropped. Subsequently, the guarantee by the guarantor powers was converted into a clause whereby the *Czechs* would be held responsible for the evacuation. That appears to be the only occasion on which the point was so much as mentioned. (See *DBFP*, ii, pp. 630–5 and *DGFP*, ii, pp. 1003–8.)

[76] *DBFP*, ii, p. 630.

The quarrel between Poland and Czechoslovakia was over Teschen, a small area (1,300 square kilometres and 300,000 inhabitants) which had effectively poisoned relations between the two states since 1920. The issue was a classic instance of the genre. Arguments about Teschen tended to reach back to Casimir the Great. The precise population structure was unclear and greatly disputed.[77] A fairly important railway line (Bogumin–Teschen) ran through the territory and there were sizeable and valued coal deposits. But it was still a very small affair and its detachment from Czechoslovakia as demanded by the Poles could by no stretch of the imagination be likened in its probable effects to that of the Sudetenland. Accordingly, what matters within the present context is rather how the Teschen dispute affected Czechoslovakia's decision on the terms of the Munich Agreement—all the more so as in explaining the decision, after the event, the leaders of Czechoslovakia gave it great weight.[78]

The Poles had been very quick to realize that Chamberlain's visit to Berchtesgaden implied, among other things, that Western support for Czech territorial integrity was at an end and that, on the other hand, it was essential to re-stake the Polish claim before the rump Czechoslovakia was guaranteed anew. Pressure was accordingly whipped up in the middle of the month and on 16 September the Polish ambassador was making it clear to Halifax that, in their view, 'any concessions extended to the German minority in Czechoslovakia should also be extended to the Poles'.[79] When they thought a plebiscite was impending they demanded a plebiscite; when it appeared that direct cession was contemplated, they asked for direct cession.[80] Given the extreme narrowness of the Polish diplomatic horizon, it cannot be denied that their tactics had a firm, internal logic. They were undoubtedly intent on getting their way; there is no reason to suppose that they did not mean what they said when they threatened to take the region by force, if need be. However, they proposed limited warfare for a limited purpose. Unlike the Germans, it was no part of their purpose to destroy the Czech state. If, incidentally, they were helping to do so, that—in the mind of

[77] Vastly different figures were offered. Two facts emerge fairly clearly: the Polish population amounted to less than half the population; and, on the other hand, there were more Poles than Czechs.

[78] See below. The Hungarians also made claims on Czechoslovak territory, following a roughly similar procedure to that of the Poles. But theirs was from the first somewhat less bellicose in tone, they were weaker militarily, and any action on their part might have revivified the Little Entente. Finally, the Magyar pressure was never ascribed the same weight as the Polish by the Czechs themselves. On the other hand, the behaviour of the Hungarians did nothing to improve Czech morale.

[79] *DBFP*, iii, p. 3.   [80] *DBFP*, iii, p. 7.

Colonel Beck, the Foreign Minister—was unfortunate; but it was by no means his aim.

Yet it was not until after the acceptance of the Anglo-French Proposals, on 22 September, that President Beneš became really alarmed at the Polish moves. Conceivably, it was not until then that he and his principal advisers had sufficiently recovered from the heavy pressure of the preceding days to take stock of other developments. At all events, on that day the Czechs did two things. Their first step was to inform the Russians of the Polish troop concentrations and movements and point out, at the same time, that 'It would therefore be desirable if Moscow would draw Warsaw's attention to the fact that the Soviet–Polish Non-Aggression Pact ceases to be valid the moment Poland attacks Czechoslovakia.'[81]

The following day, in a harshly worded Note, the Russians did just that and three days later (26 September) published its text in *Izvestia*.[82] The Poles replied irritably that they were sole judges of any action they might think necessary to take and that they could read the text of their engagements as well as the Russians.[83] Colonel Beck informed the German Ambassador that he 'attached no importance to this step', but the Ambassador, in his dispatch, hinted that he thought this an exaggeration.[84]

The second step taken by the Czechs was to agree upon and draft a letter—from Beneš to the Polish President Mościcki—which in effect conceded Teschen to the Poles, subject to an orderly procedure, in exchange for benevolent neutrality in respect of the Czechs' major conflict with the Germans. However, the decision to *dispatch* the letter seems not to have been taken until 25 September and it was not delivered until the 26th.[85] In view of the tension this was an extraordinary delay and can only be explained by assuming a parallel Czech decision to postpone the commitment to cede Teschen until it was thought entirely unavoidable. Beneš himself was later to say that it was sent simultaneously with the signing of the mobilization decree and when he believed his country would be at war with Germany in two or three days, the object being to secure Polish neutrality.[86] However, the Poles lost no time in rejecting the offer and instead, on 27 September, put forward their own 'Godesberg' terms: immediate cession. And they backed their peremptory

[81] *New Documents*, p. 112. [82] *New Documents*, p. 113.
[83] *DBFP*, iii, p. 24; and *DGFP*, p. 898. [84] *DGFP*, ii, p. 922.
[85] This emerges from a comparison of the Notes with the information in the British and German Documents. The full series of Notes exchanged between the Czechs and the Poles is published, as indicated, in L. B. Namier, *Europe in Decay*.
[86] Letter from Beneš to Namier in L. B. Namier, op. cit., p. 284, and see Namier, p. 227, fn. 1.

demand with the deployment of ten divisions of their troops along the Czechoslovak frontier.[87] It was only on 30 September (internal evidence suggests it was drafted *before* the decision on the Munich Agreement was taken) that the Czechs dispatched their reply. They offered the Poles most of what they had asked for, but still insisted on an orderly procedure to be terminated by 1 December 1938.[88]

This was the situation in Prague when the Munich terms were presented for their 'plain acceptance'. During all this time the Czechs were under considerable pressure from the Western powers to concede to the Poles what they had conceded to the Germans. There was parallel pressure on the Poles to stay their hand. Polish intransigence caused great irritation in Paris and London,[89] but the irritation had no effect on Warsaw.

The Germans encouraged the Poles (and the Hungarians) to press their claims, by force if necessary.[90] Military information and maps were exchanged between Polish and German army representatives and it was agreed that misunderstandings and encroachment by one force on the other's territory must be avoided. But it was understood that Poland must act independently of Germany and, if anything, the Germans were worried lest Polish independence be maintained even at the cost of reduced co-operation with Germany.[91] The joint conduct of operations remained at a tactical, even technical level. There is nothing whatsoever to indicate that German–Polish collusion went or was meant to go further than that. It is not conceivable that the Poles, once their own demands were satisfied, would have joined the Germans in a general military onslaught on Czechoslovakia.

So for all the bitterness with which the Czechs regarded the Polish claim, put forward in their weakest hour, they very properly never allowed themselves to be distracted by it from their fundamental preoccupation with Germany. On the contrary, they had gone a stage further in their concessions to the Poles (by undertaking to evacuate by a specified date) than in their concessions to the Germans. It could even be argued that they had gone a great deal further, in as

[87] Namier, op cit., p. 300.

[88] Once again, the Poles rejected this. They replied the same day (30 September) with an ultimatum demanding immediate evacuation of Teschen by the Czechs. Finally, the Czechs capitulated and the Poles entered Teschen a day after the Germans entered the Sudetenland.

[89] See, for example, Halifax's telegram to Kennard (ambassador in Warsaw), *DBFP*, iii, pp. 59–60; and Gamelin, *Servir*, ii, pp. 356–7.

[90] Among the evidence: *Documents and Materials Relating to the Eve of the Second World War*, Moscow, i, 1948, pp. 176–83 and 219–25. (Reports by Lipski, Polish Ambassador in Berlin, to Colonel Beck.)

[91] *DGFP*, ii, pp. 952–3 and 973–4.

much as in the case of the Sudetenland they had accepted an Anglo-French plan, not a German one, and this was conditional on guarantees, while the German demands made at Godesberg had already been rejected. It was thus possible, within the logic of the situation as it presented itself on 25 or 26 September and equally the situation on 30 September, to make a concession to the Poles and yet reject the Munich terms. In fact, until the actual presentation of the Munich terms, when war was thought very likely, such a method of obtaining Polish neutrality had been envisaged.[92] Capitulation to the Poles while rejecting Munich itself would certainly have angered the Germans beyond belief, but since rejection of Munich meant war in any case, this could hardly be a decisive consideration.[93]

A second point that emerges is that a refusal to make any further concession to the Poles would still have left the Czechs with the Russians to fall back on. The Soviet reaction to the Czechs' alarm was as swift and unequivocal as could be asked for in the circumstances. It is just possible too that the Russians would have welcomed the opportunity (presented by a Polish attack on Czechoslovakia) to anticipate by a year their subsequent invasion of Poland, under more honourable circumstances and in better company.[94]

Either way, the argument that the decision to capitulate to the great powers hinged on the ineluctability of capitulation to the Poles is inherently untenable.

(7) The differences between the Munich terms and those of the Godesberg Memorandum—which the Czechs had quickly and firmly rejected—were extremely small, hardly amounting to more than technical or even cosmetic improvements.[95] To Chamberlain they mattered, however, because he believed they implied the continued reign of international order, as opposed to anarchy. But from

[92] See also *DBFP*, iii, p. 43, showing that the Czechs distinguished between Poland, whose attitude they felt could be modified by concessions, and Hungary, which was 'too far committed to Germany and to Warsaw'.

[93] There is a suggestion (in *DBFP*, iii, p. 46) that the Czech military authorities wanted to retain the area until all threat of war had passed because of the strategic importance of the railway passing through it. Yet the map indicates that the loss of the railway would have cut off Teschen itself and, in the event of the Poles maintaining neutrality, left access to the German border areas largely unaffected.

[94] See Gamelin's conversation with the Soviet Military Attaché, in Gamelin, *Servir*, ii, p. 348.

[95] The Germans made three concessions: (*a*) Czechoslovakia would be represented on the International Commission at Berlin; (*b*) there could be, exceptionally, departures from the rule of strictly 'ethnographic determination' of the zones which are to be transferred without plebiscite'; (*c*) the complete evacuation of certain areas could be postponed by up to ten days.

the Czech point of view, the only significant comparison could be with the Anglo-French Proposals. Ten days earlier it could at least be argued that although the issue before them was one of a very severe loss of national territory, wealth, and defensive capacity, it was possible that the operation would be followed by renewed health. Now this simply could not be believed. To accept the *diktat* from Munich was not merely to bow to the threatened application of superior force; it was to renounce the material possibility of resistance to force in the future. All that could replace the lost material instrumentalities was, at best, the hope that somehow, some day, the nation would outlive its enemies.

It is noteworthy that the decision to capitulate was taken in a matter of hours. Considering the limited time available and the tremendous emotional pressures to which the Czech leaders were subject, any measured, totally rational examination of the position in which they found themselves and of the alternative policies open to them was clearly out of the question. The text of the Agreement was received at a quarter past six in the morning. The Germans did not require an answer, but they notified the Czechs that their representatives on the International Commission were to appear at 5 p.m. the same day at the Berlin Foreign Ministry. The party leaders began a meeting with President Beneš at 9.30 a.m. and the Cabinet met elsewhere at the same time. Shortly afterwards both groups, joined by the members of Dr. Hodža's late government and two generals representing the army, met together under the President's leadership. But if they believed they had until the afternoon to decide they were soon disillusioned. The British, French, and Italian envoys called and demanded a reply by noon that day. So at noon, barely two-and-a-half hours after the convening of the meeting, the decision to accept the terms was taken.[96]

Just before this meeting Beneš telephoned the Soviet minister, Alexandrovsky. He informed him of the Agreement and defined the Czech dilemma as the choice between 'beginning war with Germany, having against her Britain and France, at any rate in the sense of the attitude of their governments which are also working on the public mind getting it to believe that Czechoslovakia is the cause of the war, or capitulating to the aggressor'. Leaving open the question of the decision Czechoslovakia would take, the President wanted to know the attitude of the Soviet Union to these two possibilities: further struggle or capitulation.[97] An answer was requested by 6–7 p.m. However, at noon the Soviet envoy was informed that no answer would be required. Reporting this, in turn, Alexandrovsky added:

[96] Ripka, *Munich: Before and After*, p. 230.
[97] *New Documents*, pp. 126–7.

From the words and behaviour of Smutný and General Husárek, whom I also met at the Castle, I have no doubt that Beneš made no reference to the fact that he had received no answer from the U.S.S.R. Just the contrary. He and the Left group of the Government evidently acted on the assumption that the U.S.S.R. would come to their assistance at the first opportunity. This is borne out by yesterday's broadcast by Minister Vavrečka and the former Minister . . . Dérer who for the first time publicly announced that the U.S.S.R. was the only one who remained a loyal ally of Czechoslovakia to the end. A similar statement, but not over the radio, was made by Beran, the leader of the Agrarians. All three took part in the said meeting of Ministers.[98]

It thus appears that the question of invoking Soviet aid was never seriously discussed and the doctrine laying down that the Soviet Alliance must be contingent upon an effective alliance with the West cannot have been seriously challenged. Nor was the military situation discussed, except in the limited sense that the generals were asked questions, the answers to which could be used to support arguments advanced on other grounds.[99]

The decisive confrontation between those who supported capitulation and those who opposed it took place *after* the official decision to capitulate had been made. A deputation of six senior generals of the Czech army called on President Beneš (who was also Supreme Commander). It was composed of the Chief of the General Staff, General Krejci, three provincial commanders, the Inspector-General of the Forces, and the Prime Minister, General Syrový.

The generals argued that the troops were already mobilized and deployed in the fortified areas and that, in consequence, this was the time to resist, if ever. They were convinced that the population would resist, even if the government did not. 'We must go to war,' they said, 'regardless of consequences. The Western powers will be forced to follow us. The population of the Republic is united, the army is resolute, anxious to fight. And even if we were left alone we must not yield; the army has the duty to defend the national territory, wants to go and will go to war.'[100]

---

[98] Telegram dated 1 October. *New Documents*, pp. 130–1. The editor of the *New Documents* points out that both telegrams, the one containing Beneš's question, the other cancelling it, failed to reach Moscow until the late afternoon. From the telegram just quoted it emerges that this was due to difficulties of transmission. However, the Czechs never denied their knowledge or belief that the Russians were prepared to assist them. Thus, Dr. Hubert Ripka in 'The Repudiation of Munich', *Czechoslovak Documents and Sources*, no. 6, 1943: 'Soviet policy was prepared to implement its formal treaty pledges to us.' At the time of writing Dr. Ripka was a minister of state in the Czechoslovak government in exile.

[99] 'Pierre Buk', *La Tragédie tchécoslovaque*, op. cit., p. 151.

[100] Edvard Beneš, *Mnichovske dny*, London, 1955, pp. 115–17, quoted in

'They begged, entreated, threatened. Some of them wept.'[101]
President Beneš admired them and sympathized, as he later recounted, but refused to reconsider. He gave three reasons. The first
related to the central fact of the French *de facto* denunciation of their
Treaty of Alliance. The second related to the Polish threat to occupy
Teschen, with the military and political implications of fighting two
enemies. The third reason related, quite simply, to the foreseeable
slaughter.[102] But

War will come quickly, [the President told them] Great Britain, France
and the other nations will not help us fight now, but they will certainly
have to fight later—perhaps—under worse conditions. We would not be
understood by Europe and the world if we provoked the war now. The
nation must endure. Do not give way, whatever happens, and wait for the
right moment. Then we shall enter the struggle again, as we did in 1914.
And we shall win again. [103]

Finally,

The generals left dissatisfied, embittered, and in a desperate mood. And
as for me, I pondered seriously once more the question: Have I made the
right decision in this terrible crisis?[104]

Thus it may be seen that the decision to accept the Munich terms
was taken quickly and under the heaviest kind of pressure. There was
none of the careful, if anguished, deliberation which characterized
the lengthy discussions that preceded the acceptance of the Anglo-
French Proposals. There are no signs of preparation—except mental
and perhaps unconscious—for the blow. The only hint of a discussion of alternative policies is to be found in the confrontation between
the President and the generals and it is characteristic that it took
place on the generals' initiative, not the government's.[105] With one
exception, the arguments that appear to have been advanced by
Beneš and those hinted at by Syrový in his broadcast message to the

Otakar Odlozik, 'Edvard Beneš on Munich Days', *Journal of Central European Affairs*, xvi, January 1957.
[101] Speech by President Beneš at Chicago, 27 May 1943, quoted in B. Bílek, *Fifth Column at Work*, 1945, p. 75.
[102] Beneš, *Mnichovske dny*, pp. 115–17. What was said in detail, under these headings, is unknown.
[103] Bílek, *Fifth Column at Work*, p. 75.
[104] Beneš, *Mnichovske dny*, pp. 115–17.
[105] The first occasion on which President Beneš, or anyone else who was in a position to know, revealed that there had been disagreement between the generals and himself, was in a speech delivered in London on 8 January 1941. But, naturally enough, few hard facts were offered and the operative statement was that, 'for Czechoslovakia to proceed alone would have been ... either supreme desperation or just a vain gesture'. See 'Why Czechoslovakia did not fight' in *The Central European Observer*, 17 January 1941.

public[106] were based—at best—on half truths. The defence of
Czechoslovakia was far from being a desperate undertaking. It was
certainly not 'hopeless'. And to say categorically, as General Syrový
did, that resistance 'would have meant the sacrifice not only of an
entire generation of our adult men, but also of women and children',[107] was greatly to exaggerate. So far as the Poles were concerned ('our neighbours to the north'), by 30 September the
question had been settled in principle. From the Czech point of
view, it had been done with the deliberate purpose of obtaining
Polish neutrality. The case of Teschen was neither so vital to the
state nor so sound a one (from the formal point of view) that it could
not be sacrificed in the interests of avoiding a greater sacrifice.
Finally, the Czechs had not been entirely deserted. They had no
reason to believe that the Russians would not continue to support
them, politically, possibly by exerting pressure on Poland, if in
no other way. It was by their own decision that they denied themselves the opportunity to invoke Soviet aid. In the face of this,
discussion as to whether the Rumanians would or would not have
allowed Soviet forces through their territory or airspace or whether
in fact transport facilities were or were not adequate[108] becomes
meaningless.

There remains the one—unanswerable—argument that resistance
implied slaughter. No doubt the Czech leaders could not have foreseen what the German occupation of Bohemia and Moravia would
be like. Perhaps they envisaged a new version, admittedly somewhat
more brutal, of Habsburg rule. Even such a regime is really not
comparable in terms of the physical pain it inflicts on the population
with what is suffered in war. The dread of a great disaster and a
national blood-letting was very strong in Prague, and most under-
standably so. Yet there can be no doubt that they would have gone
to war without any such reservations had the Western powers been
with them, even though for many months and as far as the mind
could calculate, it would have been the same fighting against very
nearly the same odds. 'Nous n'attendons pas un nouvel Austerlitz,

---

[106] The key points made by Syrový were:
[First:] We had the choice between a desperate and hopeless defence . . . and the
acceptance of conditions . . . unparalleled in history for ruthlessness.
[Second:] . . . we were deserted, and we stood alone.
[Third:] All the states of Europe, including our neighbours to the north and
south, are under arms. We are in a certain sense a fortress beleaguered by forces
which are more powerful than ours.
(RIIA, *Documents on International Affairs, 1938*, ii, p. 327.)
[107] Ibid.
[108] Cf. G. F. Kennan, *Russia and the West under Lenin and Stalin*, Boston,
1961, pp. 323–4.

une armée française en Moravie. Nous tiendrons le coup nous-mêmes, le temps qu'il faudra, des semaines, des mois, quatre, six peut-être,' Beneš had told Henri Hauser only a few months before.[109]

Like all civilized men of his generation, Beneš hated and feared war. But war in good company, in an honourable cause, and with every prospect of injecting additional cement into the national and international foundations of the state—was one thing. War conducted alone, with uncertain prospects, or war in the company of one barbarian state against another—was very different. For the Czechs, with their historic defeat in the seventeenth century in mind and their newly re-won and still fragile sovereign status, such a prospect was particularly terrible. The cruelty of their position lay in the fact that the only way they themselves could act to preserve their national sovereignty—to be lost, in any case, after Munich—was by endangering it in a harsh and bloody departure from their political and moral norms.

(8) The case of Czechoslovakia in 1938 was thus paradoxical. In certain respects it was an easily demonstrable model of what a small, enlightened nation could do to maximize its resources. Economically, it was quite strong. Politically, it was for many years the centre of a system of alliances which was anchored to the French, to be sure, but which owed much of its strength and inspiration to the Czechs themselves. Militarily, it was capable of producing a machine that in the moment of crisis was a match for the adversary's. That Czechoslovakia's economic strength availed it nothing in the crisis is only natural: economic potential can be significant only as the basis of extended build-up of forces or as support in a lengthy conflict. But the Czech alliances melted the moment they were tested or were left uninvoked; and the military machine played no role of any kind in the defence of the state and only barely in the calculations of the political leaders.

How this situation arose and what alternatives faced the Czech leaders even as late as September 1938, has been described. Had they been less fixed in their minds as to the policy they should pursue and more unwilling from the start to pay the price and make the concessions demanded of them, it is possible that the situation facing them on 30 September would never have arisen in the first place. It would certainly have been different in outline, significantly so. Had they decided on war when all other possibilities were exhausted there is no reason to believe their defeat was certain; on the contrary, they had every prospect of maintaining an effective resistance extended over a considerable period and the entire European situation would most

[109] Hauser, in *L'Année politique française et étrangère*, xiv, 1939.

probably have been altered thereby, as Hitler understood from the first. Within the logic of what the Czechoslovak leaders had been trying to do for twenty years, the most that can be said is that having recognized the failure of their policy, they accepted defeat and resolved to preserve their nation physically, until 'as in 1914 ... we shall win again'. In terms of humanity and private morality this argument was clearly unanswerable. But in terms of the practical management of affairs winning 'as in 1914' meant Czechoslovakia's total and unmitigated dependence on foreign political forces beyond its control and only marginally, if at all, susceptible to its influence. It came very close to the abnegation of statehood and the abdication of sovereignty.

It is difficult to escape the impression that in Prague these grave and heartrending matters of state were discussed and understood within an extremely rigid framework of ideas. Czechoslovakia must be linked to the West; Czechoslovakia must not fight alone; Czechoslovakia must not enter into an effective relationship with the Soviet Union unaccompanied by France; Czechoslovakia must preserve its reputation, even when the behaviour of other powers belies theirs; and so on. All those principles had strong roots in history and in good sense. Employed together as a system of rules for political conduct they could only lead to disaster.

Another question that arises is whether President Beneš was not right after all in seeing or sensing that Czechoslovak sovereignty had too small a base to be real or durable; that it could only be conditional on the backing and approval of much larger, truly powerful and sovereign units; that the sovereignty of the Czech state was only effective in the domestic sphere (where the Czechs were, in fact, capable of very strong and determined measures), while in the international arena they were in a state of vassalage. How else can his own final, public judgement on his stewardship be understood except as founded on such a view?

I only wish to make it clear that in the years 1936–38 Czechoslovak policy rightly diagnosed what was the matter with Europe. It did everything, really everything, to retrieve the situation of Czechoslovakia, of its friends and of all Europe in the face of Fascist gangsterism and pan-German Nazism and of war itself.

In that period when the European and world crisis was approaching, there was no State in Europe which could have a clearer conscience of doing its duty towards its Nation and its friends than the Czechoslovak Republic under the presidency of Masaryk and myself.[110]

The case of Beneš's Czechoslovakia calls attention to the common truth that over and beyond the complex interplay between the

[110] Beneš, *Memoirs*, p. 33.

human and material resources available to a government and the nature of the internal and external opposition to it, the capacity to pursue an autonomous national policy with any measure of success is a function of the will of the national leaders to do so. For while the outcome of any conflict—and *a fortiori* of an armed conflict—obviously depends, in the first instance, on the balance of objective and intrinsic attributes of the parties to the conflict, where the will to employ those attributes is lacking, or where it is paralysed by the apparent disproportion of relative strength, or for any other reason such as the private qualities and views of the leaders, there military and industrial strength and other objective attributes will avail nothing. They are, in any case, only a potential.

The management of a state so placed seems to require a special firmness and a blindness to all considerations extraneous to the over-riding consideration of survival. First-generation leaders of a 'new nation'—as Beneš and his colleagues were at the time—because they will have spent many years arguing their case in other nations' chancelleries, are not always fully aware of this. When they are, their initial instinct is often to deny it. Moreover, they often tend to remain in awe of the great powers, even to the extent of privately disparaging their own formal equality with them. Given this frame of mind, the full range of political and military possibilities available to them is unlikely to be surveyed, still less exploited.

The case of Israel in its contemporary conflict with the Soviet Union—increasingly the crucial (and, for Israel, conceivably the decisive) aspect of the unending Middle East war—bears comparison with that of Czechoslovakia's conflict with the Germans and yet is sharply different in a number of ways. Not merely is the structure of the Middle East conflict as a whole vastly more intricate than that with which Beneš and his colleagues attempted to cope over thirty years ago, but the frame of mind in which successive governments of Israel have approached the external opposition to them is almost a mirror image of the Czechs'. For it cannot be said of the Israelis—nor of the Arabs, for that matter—that what they lack is firmness of purpose and the requisite degree of blindness to all considerations extraneous to the overriding consideration of survival.

CHAPTER THREE

Israel—the Contemporary Paradigm

The question as to whether a tertiary power can face a primary power in a conflict which either tends or might tend to war, has ceased to be one which can be broken down into a comparison, however detailed, of available material resources. No state can conceivably withstand the onslaught of a contemporary primary power's nuclear forces, not even another primary power. It seems probable, moreover, that no minor state can withstand the full onslaught of such a power's purely conventional forces. But even if it could, the prospect of defeat in a conventional war to which it has been *fully* committed is one which, it must be assumed, no primary power could accept. Nuclear forces would therefore be employed, or their employment threatened, if the conventional battles went against them. Thus in the contemporary world a duel on the hypothetical German–Czechoslovak model is extremely difficult to conceive. And, in fact, where modern primary powers are in conflict with tertiary powers the participation of the major power is invariably mitigated and the conflict is possible, which is to say, pursuable over a period, only because the major disputant is less than fully and directly committed. The most instructive contemporary paradigm thus tends to be a study in complexity—in the mitigation of power and the indirect application of resources. It remains that within the complexity there is, as it were, an immanent duel.

As the following discussion of the contemporary Middle East war attempts to show, this complexity arises from the fact that conflict between states, in such a case, is pursued by two distinct *classes* of powers on two distinct levels or *tiers*. It is the interconnection between the two tiers of conflict that is largely at the basis of the conflict between members of different classes (in the present case: the tertiary power Israel and the primary power Russia). But equally, it is the intercalation of the two tiers which is wholly at the basis of the moderating mechanism in default of which the forcible resolution of the issue between them would have been effected long ago. It follows that neither of the levels on which the Middle East conflict is being played out can be considered paramount or more important than the other. Each will be considered in turn.

Arabs and Jews

(1) The peculiar complexity and intractability of the conflict between Arabs and Jews in the Middle East stem, in the final analysis, from the twin circumstances that neither the substance of the conflict nor the parties engaged in it are really susceptible to agreed and straightforward definition. The identity of the parties, the instrumental and ultimate goals they have set themselves, the means by which their goals are pursued, the methods whereby allies are recruited and enemies repulsed—all those tend to vary from time to time and from place to place. The one feature of real permanence and regularity is the depth of the emotional and ideological involvement of those who happen to be immediately caught up in the conflict. Otherwise it is the disparity of structure and the irregularity and impermanence of the membership, capabilities, and behaviour of each camp that have endured most strikingly. Whether viewed synoptically from any single point upon the immense time-scale of Jewish–Arab relations since the emergence of Islam, or diachronically along it as the conflict has fluctuated and evolved, it is the extraordinary asymmetry of the facts of the conflict on either side and the incompatibility of respective perceptions of it that are impressive.

One consequence of these disparities and of the perpetual change which the structure and identity of the conflict undergo is the lack of even minimal consensus in the folklore and the polemical literature under which the subject is now buried. But the confusion and contradictions in the great mountain of interpretations and chronicles of the conflict that has been growing steadily since the end of the First World War do more than typify it. What is thought, said, and written about the conflict, to say nothing of what is sensed or felt intuitively, is of the greatest possible importance not only for an understanding of it, but for its direct impact on the conflict itself. In an important sense, the argument about its nature and dynamics *is* the conflict, at any rate where the immediate parties are concerned. The passion and dedication with which views are held and enunciated are among the principal forces impelling the parties to act upon, or resist, each other. And because there has been no slackening of the tendency of the parties to ascribe vast, even supreme significance to the conflict, or more properly, *to the conflict as they understand it*, and because the concrete actions each has taken have had the effect of greatly reinforcing and heightening the other's most extreme interpretations and bitterest fears, its broad evolution has been along lines of ever greater commitment, ever higher stakes, and ever heavier and more widespread social, political, economic, and, of course, military involvement.

In the event, at each major stage and turn, Arabs and Jews have found themselves confronted by a situation which appeared to them —which is to say, to all but socially and politically insignificant minorities within each camp—to offer a choice between radically abandoning the previously accepted view of the conflict or persevering with redoubled efforts to impose a solution that would accord with it. But to abandon the view of the conflict to which one had been committed was—and remains—in each case tantamount to the abandonment of a certain view of self and society. And such an abandonment has come to entail for the members of both camps, but for quite different reasons, a sacrifice ever more difficult to contemplate each time that circumstances have impelled (or been held to impel) even minimal consideration of the question.

There are thus some grounds for seeing the conflict in its totality as a conflict of ideologies—unless 'ideology' is too grand a term to apply to what are, in fact, hardly more than sets of fairly simple, often imperfectly articulated, views and judgements on the conflict itself, on the nature and structure of one's own side and (more particularly) of the opponent's, and what is, as opposed to what ideally should be, the state of relations between them. The main consequence of each side's understanding of the conflict (and of each other) is that there can be neither agreement on its substance, nor *a fortiori* progress towards its resolution, without a profound transformation in the nature and structure of one side or the other.

(2) The identity and purposes of the disputants can, in principle, be discussed on at least four levels: first, at the quasi-objective level of active and potential *material* involvement; secondly, at the level of the terms in which each side sees itself; thirdly, at the level of the terms in which each side sees the other; and fourthly, at the level of behaviour in concrete and, above all, critical situations. All levels are significant, but not in isolation from each other. It is, in fact, the intricate and irregular relationship between all four that must be grasped before all else.

At the initial level of analysis matters are relatively straightforward. There have been shifts and changes from time to time, some of them of great importance. But it is not impossible by the normal means of historical and political inquiry to distinguish those placed in the inner circle of direct conflict from those placed in the outer circles who offer no more than political and material support in one degree or another, or, at the very least, are capable of rocking the boat, but, equally, may refrain from doing so.

Fifty years ago the Jewish settler community in Palestine and the Zionist movement which promoted and backed them could by no stretch of the imagination be seen as representative of more than a minority of world Jewry. The Zionists were intent upon a colossal re-structuring of the Jewish people along entirely fresh social and economic lines. The fundamental item of their analysis and pro-gramme was the absolute necessity, as they saw it, of re-establishing the Jews as a nation with political capabilities—in other words, a state—and of promoting and defending Jewish national interests first and foremost through independent political and, if necessary, military instrumentalities, rather than by the age-old techniques of lobbying, remonstrance, and the rendering of services in exchange for immediate or future protection. Like all revolutionaries with a serious, and therefore disturbing, case to argue, they were for the most part resisted or ignored for a very long while. But today their position in Jewry as a whole is transformed. On the one hand, the State of Israel exists and acts and is equipped with independent instruments of policy beyond the wildest dreams of its forerunners. And on the other hand, active opposition to the state, which is to say, to the Zionist programme, has practically disappeared among Jews and is limited to veritable fringe groups. The latter are of two varieties: the hyper-religious and the adepts of universalistic, usually ultra-leftist, creeds. The first offers retreat to the Middle Ages. The second purports to offer release from the dilemmas of Jewish identity altogether. Thus neither group is in a position to appeal to, let alone act for, the bulk of Jewry.

The origins of this great change constitute too broad a subject to be dealt with here. But it may be pertinent to recall that few Jews, regardless of their circumstances, could remain indifferent to four major events of our period: the physical liquidation of almost the whole of Central and Eastern-European Jewry by the Germans; the establishment of Israel itself; the rise of the Jewish population of Israel through the Ingathering of the Exiles and through natural increase to the point where it constitutes the third (possibly the second) largest Jewish community anywhere and is, for a host of reasons, the natural focus of all Jewish cultural and religious activity; and finally, the trauma of May/June 1967—the prelude to, and the conduct and outcome of the third Arab–Jewish war. At all events, the immediate consequence of this great shift in the central currents of Jewish opinion has been to reduce almost to a nullity the old distinction between Zionist and non-Zionist Jews. For a Jew to be anti-Zionist today is to be, in a profound sense, retrograde, self-

E

contradictory, apostatical and, in the extreme case, disloyal. In short, it is to cut oneself off from what has become the central Jewish cause. Certainly it is not difficult to find individuals, members of the Western European and North American intellectual communities in particular, who have done just that. But they carry little political or economic weight and are too remote from the vital arena of the conflict to affect it seriously, apart from providing a measure of moral comfort to the other side. The really crucial contemporary distinction among Jews is rather between those who are directly involved in the Middle East conflict, viz. the nationals and inhabitants of Israel, and those who are not, and whose attitudes are therefore free to range all the way from complete emotional and intellectual identification with the Israelis to polite indifference to their fate.

The Arab camp has experienced a parallel, in some ways still more intense, drawing of lines—with the acceptance of the conflict as a central national issue in the sense that for an Arab *qua* Arab to fail to support the cause is to be profoundly disloyal to his people. This has long been the case, but it was not always so. It may be worth recalling that in 1919 the most considerable spokesman for the Arab world of the time, the Emir Feisal of Hejaz, was prepared to tell the Paris Peace Conference that Palestine 'for its universal character should be left on one side for the mutual consideration of all parties interested'—among whom the Jews obviously figured. Moreover, Feisal specifically agreed with the Zionists in a famous written memorandum that 'in the establishment of the Constitution and Administration of Palestine, all such measures shall be adopted as will afford the fullest guarantees for carrying into effect the British Government's [Balfour] Declaration of November 2nd, 1917'; and that 'all necessary measures shall be taken to encourage and stimulate immigration of Jews into Palestine on a large scale, and as quickly as possible to settle Jewish immigrants on the land through closer settlement and intensive cultivation of the soil.'[1]

Feisal's most probable purpose was to recruit Jewish support for his independent Greater Syria project and he added a proviso to the effect that the Agreement would be void if his major plans were incapable of fulfilment. In his eyes Palestine was a special case and he believed that Arab political interests in it could be properly subordinated to the general purpose of achieving independence for the Arab heartland.

Today, the Weizmann–Feisal Agreement cannot but be rated a curiosity of history and Palestine is very far from being seen as a

[1] Paragraphs Three and Four of the Weizmann–Feisal Agreement, 3 January 1919.

special case to which other Arab interests may properly be subordinated. And as the question of formal political independence for
Arab lands as a whole has long been solved, Palestine necessarily
remains in Arab eyes the lone—and therefore the great and unacceptable—exception. As for the Palestine Arabs themselves, it
became clear by the 1920s that they were unalterably opposed to the
establishment of first a Jewish majority in the country and then a
Jewish state. And the closer the Jews appeared to come to their goal
the sharper became the general resistance of the Palestinian Arabs to
them. Finally, the sharper the conflict in and over Palestine, the more
other Arab communities came to be drawn into it.

Here and there in the Arab parts of the Middle East there have
remained some small, informal pockets of scepticism and less than
wholehearted support for the general crusade against Israel seen as a
cause in which all Arabs are concerned. In Egypt and Lebanon
notably, but also in the Maghreb, there has always been a current of
what might be termed local nationalist or particularist opinion
running contrary to the now preponderant pan-Arab trend. It is still
alive.[2] But such dissent from pan-Arabism does not neccessarily
mean—in fact, very rarely means—explicit dissent on the specific
issue of Israel. And where it does it is neither organized nor institutionalized. On this subject it is the official policies and ideologies
alone that are supported and voiced and which alone have general
social respectability. And they are such as will admit no real deviation.
State and society are for all practical purposes at one here. Thus, as
in the Jewish world, what really matters is the extent and intensity
of positive support for the cause which may, indeed, vary from mere
lip-service to the most ardent participation at the front.

The basic difference between the Jewish and Arab camps in this
context is a structural one. The overwhelming majority of Arabs are
subjects of Arab governments. The overwhelming majority of Jews
are subjects of non-Jewish governments. To put the same point
somewhat differently, membership of the Jewish camp, not only for
purposes connected with the Arab–Israel conflict, but for many, if
not all, others as well, is predominantly voluntary. Membership of
the Arab camp is not. This difference has the consequence that in
strict and concrete terms the human and material resources available
to Israel and under its unquestioned authority and therefore, by
extension, the diplomatic and military resources on which it can
count at all times, have always been and no doubt will always be
substantially inferior to those available to the Arab governments.

[2] On the revival of Egyptian (as opposed to Arab) nationalism in the wake of
the 1967 war see, for example, Ibn al Asal (pseud.), 'Return to Cairo', *Encounter*,
August 1969.

The quantitative disparity is marked even where only the resources of those Arab governments which are actively involved in significant military conflict are compared with Israel's.[3] But against this must be set Israel's advantages: qualitatively superior military manpower, interior lines of communication, a more effective command structure, and so forth.

What both sides have in common, however, is the fact that each consists of a multitude of independent participants placed, as it were, in a series of concentric circles such that active involvement in any given case will vary more or less with the distance from the centre; and that it is those centrally placed whose behaviour and interaction give the conflict its underlying dynamic and its essential structure. The centrally placed participants—Israel, Egypt, and (in rough descending order of political and military importance) Syria, Jordan, Iraq, Libya, Algeria, Saudi Arabia, Lebanon, and Sudan—are not oblivious to, nor can they fully depend upon their allies—respectively the various Jewish communities outside Israel and the other Arab governments. But it is they and not their allies who determine at the margin how each camp will act as a whole and it is on them that the attention of all concerned, whether within the broad circle of the conflict itself or outside it altogether, is rightly focused.

The exceptional case is that of the Palestine Arabs themselves. The end of the first (1947–9) Arab–Jewish war found the Palestinians in almost total political and social disarray. They themselves had taken only a small part in it: the major fighting was between the Jews and the regular Arab armies of Egypt, Syria, Iraq, and Jordan which had moved into Palestine to forestall and, failing that, to destroy the newly-proclaimed Israel.[4] The Arab Palestinian state, which the United Nations partition resolution of 1947 had provided for along with the Jewish state, was lost in the ensuing shuffle. Most of the territory set apart for it was annexed by Jordan (with British encouragement, but over the violent protests of all the other Arab states);[5] part was annexed by Israel; and a third part (the Gaza Strip) was occupied and ruled, although never formally annexed, by

---

[3] See Appendix, p. 132.

[4] 'This will be a momentous war of extermination which will be spoken of in history like the Mongolian massacres and the Crusades.' Abd al-Rahman Azzam, Secretary-General of the Arab League, BBC broadcast, 15 May 1948.

[5] Only Britain and Pakistan ever recognized the annexation *de jure*. The Arab League, after proclaiming the annexation a violation of its Charter and considering the expulsion of Jordan, eventually resolved 'to treat the Arab part of Palestine annexed by Jordan as a trust in its hands until the Palestine case is fully solved in the interests of its inhabitants'. For a detailed discussion see Y. Z. Blum, 'The Missing Reversioner: Reflections on the Status of Judea and Samaria', *Israel Law Review*, iii, 2 April 1968.

Egypt. Individually, many of the Palestine Arabs became refugees and most of these have lived ever since in a state of great hardship and still greater indignity. Some remained put and became citizens of Israel; a greater proportion became citizens of Jordan; and the rest became and have remained, in effect, stateless persons variously under the control of the Egyptians, the Syrians, and the Lebanese. Except in Jordan, the Palestinians were thus in no position anywhere to exert a measure of real influence over the governments under whose authority they had come; and even in Jordan many years passed before they began to play a really significant political role. Such political and military organizations as were set up from time to time and purported to represent them were by and large initiated and manipulated, or alternatively repressed, by their protectors.

The second (1956) Arab–Jewish war was one to the precipitation of which small groups of Palestine Arab marauders and saboteurs, inspired and largely organized by the Egyptians, certainly contributed. But in the event, it was fought as a war between Egypt and Israel and the defeat of Egypt and the subsequent interposition of United Nations forces between the two countries, served to underline the well-nigh complete dependence of the Palestine Arabs on the major Arab states, and on Egypt above all. If the Arab world was divided (Egypt had fought alone in 1956) and its greatest army incapable of crushing Israel, what remained but to work for union and build up the collective forces in anticipation of the ultimate, victorious confrontation? In the meantime it was for the Palestine Arabs to continue as wards of the Arab states.

At the start, the third (1967) Arab–Jewish war appeared likely to evolve somewhat more along the lines of the events of 1948 than on those of 1956: Arab unity was largely preserved this time and the Arab forces, collectively, were clearly great enough to overwhelm those of Israel. The defeat inflicted on the Arabs in the Six Days War was therefore all the more shattering in both real and moral terms. But, in one significant respect the results were the reverse of those of 1948, for the Palestine Arabs emerged at last as an independent, if uncertain, political factor on their own account. Ironically, their re-entry on the scene was largely made possible by Israel's occupation of all of the former British mandated territory 'Palestine', by which means the bulk of the Palestine Arabs were freed from the tutelage of the Egyptians and the Jordanians. Of great import too was the fact that the war and the events leading up to it had discredited both the Arab governments and their leading Palestinian clients and that in its aftermath, the incapacity of all concerned to reverse events by conventional military and diplomatic means was manifest. The field thus appeared free for new men to act out new and fashionable ideas

and the opportunity was rapidly seized by a host of fresh personalities and movements. The broad result has been that the Palestinians
now figure once more as a considerable, if still imperfectly definable,
politico-military factor in their own right, with complex, yet uncertain, consequences for the evolution of the conflict as a whole. It
is true that in real or military terms, they amount to hardly more
than an adjunct to the main Arab forces and that if they were denied
the safe bases offered them with varying degrees of goodwill by the
Arab states they would barely be able to operate at all. But politically
and psychologically their impact on Arab–Israel relations is once
more that of a prime catalyst and symbol of the conflict. And the fact
that they have attained a moderate degree of independence of action
means that for the first time since 1948 an organizational divergence
within the Arab camp along lines of interest, as opposed to theory
and ideology, is at least possible.

(3) A summary identification of the parties to the conflict in real
terms—i.e. in terms of actual and potential material, especially
military, participation—thus suggests that involved in it are two
untidy and uncertain coalitions of communities. One is to all intents
and purposes identical with the states which are members of the
Arab League and the associated military and political organizations
of the Palestine Arabs. The other is composed of a firm centre—
Israel—and a soft penumbra of Jewish communal and ecclesiastical
institutions and individual well-wishers in the Jewish Diaspora
around it. A discussion of the parties and their purposes on the
secondary and tertiary levels of analysis—namely, the terms in
which they see themselves and the terms in which they see their
opponents—is therefore a much more difficult undertaking. Nevertheless, only on these levels can the cement that binds these coalitions
together be found and the immensely powerful drives that fuel and
perpetuate the conflict be detected.

One key to the Arab perception of the conflict—and indeed to
their involvement in it—is the view that the Arabs constitute a single
people or nation which was, and by rights should be once more,
united. The Arab nation is seen as being endowed with unique
attributes, such as a language which is inherently superior to all
others and (its members being preponderantly Muslims) a pervasive
and collective sense of spiritual values which distinguish it from the
nations and nationalism of the West. Moreover, where

internal divisions exist, such as sects or tribes, [they] are but the result of
ignorance or of foreign interference. Add to this the claim, made with
varying degrees of conviction, that the most outstanding features of
civilization in the West have their origin in the Arab–Muslim tradition and

the peculiar feeling of being a chosen people derived from their central position in Islam, and you have all the elements from which historical constructs are constantly being devised and revised, all designed to justify aspiration and hope for the future in terms of past achievement.[6]

What matters in practice is that Arab leaders are impelled by this view to maintain a posture of unity and mutual trust, even where neither really obtains, and to accept that the familiar norms of international behaviour in respect of non-intervention by one state in the internal affairs of another, do not apply and cannot be held to apply in the Arab world.[7] On the contrary, mutual involvement and mutual responsibility are the norms and these can always be invoked, often to great effect, by those who claim to be the most catholic in their pan-Arab policies. The Syrians, for example, have made frequent use of this tactic, often to the embarrassment of other Arab governments caught in the contradictions that simultaneous, if uncertain, pursuit of both particularist and universalist goals often entail.

For all these reasons it is an established and non-contentious item of the Arab position that the Palestine issue—meaning both the fate of the Palestine Arabs *and* the fate of the former British mandated territory 'Palestine'—is the concern of all Arabs *qua* Arabs and, contrariwise, that the Palestine Arabs are entitled to call upon all other Arabs for assistance. So although the immediate matter of the contemporary conflict between Jews and Arabs in the Middle East is the Palestinian territory and its government—entirely so up until the occupation of Egyptian and Syrian areas in 1967, but still essentially so to this day—the issues cannot but be seen as affecting all Arabs. Moreover, if the loss of Palestine, once it had been identified as Arab in the Arab mind, were to be final, it could not but be judged a very cruel blow to the resurgent Arab nation. In alternative terms, acquiescence in the establishment of Israel and *a fortiori* the maintenance of amicable relations with it, could only begin to be conceivable if pan-Arabism were radically amended in content or entirely abandoned.

[6] G. E. von Grunebaum, *Modern Islam, the Search for Cultural Identity*, New-York, 1964, pp. 284–5.

[7] An example: the Egyptians were very heavily involved in the Yemeni civil war which broke out at the end of 1962 and ended eight years later. At its peak the Egyptian expeditionary force numbered no less than 68,000 men. (*The Times*, 21 December 1966, p. 9.) Smaller bodies of Egyptian troops have been sent at various times to Syria, to Iraq, Algeria, and, more recently, Libya. In each case, the object of the exercise was purely domestic or inter-Arab, i.e. to support a ruling faction against competitors or to assist one Arab state against others (specifically, Algeria against Morocco). What matters is that, from a pan-Arab point of view, there is nothing fundamentally illegitimate about such intervention, as there would be if a non-Arab state were so to intervene.

Against such a background of what is both right *and* politic for Arab leaders the third Jewish Commonwealth takes on a distinctly sinister aspect. First, because it is Jewish; secondly because it is a commonwealth, i.e. an independent political entity; thirdly because the continuing failure of the vastly more numerous and militarily, politically, and financially better-endowed Arabs to suppress it, calls into question the practicability of the one great idea or creed which offers Arabs at least a vision of something better than the present unstable and petty *kleinstaaterei*, inefficient and corrupt government, and technological and economic underdevelopment.

Despite occasional protestations to the contrary, some sincerely meant, some not, there can hardly be any question that the Arabs, as Muslims, approach Jews as Jews from a profoundly anti-Semitic standpoint.[8] Whereas the Arab as such does not really enter the Jewish historic past except in the environmental sense, the Jews, as the progenitors of all monotheists, played a minor but critical role in the origins of Islam. And as with Christianity, it is a role that is generally resented.

The Muslim tradition has it, for example, that while the Jews recognized the authenticity of Mohammed's mission, their pride and will to dominate impelled them to reject the faith. Moreover, they deceived the Prophet and attempted to frustrate him and his followers by eliminating all mention of him in their Bible. Altogether, they are a perfidious, malevolent and contemptible people, and, as is specifically foretold in the *Hadith*, their destruction will necessarily precede the Resurrection and the Last Judgement.[9] The proper attitude for Muslims to take towards the Jews is therefore one of cautious toleration—to put it at its best. But certainly there is no room here for their being accepted as in any sense equals, least of all politically. Thus the emergence of a Jewish polity in their midst would have been very difficult for the Muslims to accept in the best

---

[8] Strictly speaking, the term is an absurd one, doubly so in this case as it is improbable that more than a minority of modern Jews are Semites and entirely likely that a great many Arabs are. Nevertheless, a glance at, say, political cartoons in the Arab press (hook-nosed, humpbacked Jews, and all the rest) should suffice to justify the use of the term in its accepted, contemporary sense. 'Anti-Jewish' would be a piece of pedantry.

[9] Georges Vajda, 'Juifs et Musulmans selon le Hadit', *Journal Asiatique*, vol. 229, January–March 1937, pp. 112–13. '*Le Dajjal*, L'Antéchrist des Musulmans, comptera parmis ses adherents des Juifs. Lui vaincu, ses compagnons seront massacrés, et lorsqu'un Juif cherchera refuge sous un arbre ou une pierre, ces objets prendront la parole pour dire au Musulman: "Voici qu'un Juif est caché sous moi, tue-le!" ' Vajda, loc. cit. For a general account see S. D. Goitein, *Jews and Arabs—Their Contacts Through the Ages*, New York, 1964. Sociological surveys conducted on the West Bank shortly after the Six Days War amply confirm the vitality of these traditions.

of circumstances. That it should have occurred to the accompaniment of great failures of Arab arms and the displacement through panic flight of a great many of their brethren, goes a long way to explain their urge to proclaim Israel an embodiment of injustice and their desire to blame the catastrophe on Jewish perfidy and malevolence, rather than anything else.

In short, the Jewish character of Israel has served to intensify very greatly the hurt its establishment has caused the Arabs as well as the great and somewhat self-righteous fervour which many of them devote to the conflict and to the underlying claim that the State of Israel is an abomination that may be legitimately, indeed must be, destroyed. As the then first Vice-President of the United Arab Republic explained, during a visit to Pakistan in 1966, 'the aggressive Israeli existence is the clear embodiment of a depraved humanity which must be uprooted'.[10] It is to be noted that this has in fact been the major line of propaganda and argument on the subject in the Arab world for a great many years—particularly, but not exclusively, in the domestic sphere. It is supported by all possible technical means and it tends to rely on any material that comes to hand, not excluding that ancient forgery, the *Protocols of the Elders of Zion* (which has been disseminated in the Arab world in recent years on a massive scale).[11]

Whether and to what extent the bulk of Arab leaders and the Arab intelligentsia actually subscribe to this view of their opponent it is impossible to say. It is evident that many do, that the machinery of government fosters this view in most Arab states and denies it in none, that it is staple diet in schools and the armed forces, in the press and on the radio, and that there is abundant evidence that it falls on highly receptive ears. What matters most is that it is fundamental to the climate in which the conflict is waged. Indeed, it may well be thought the keystone of its present structure: it is to this quasi-demonological view of Israel as an evil and an aberration that must be liquidated, that the Arab leadership—Palestinian and non-Palestinian alike—have now committed themselves.[12] There is no

[10] Field Marshal Amer, quoted by Cairo Radio, 8 December 1966. There is a very full discussion of the subject in Yehoshafat Harkabi, *Emdat ha-Aravim be-Sikhsukh Israel–Arav* (The Arab Position in the Israel–Arab Conflict), Tel-Aviv, 1968.

[11] At least seven different translations of the *Protocols* into Arabic, in ten editions published in Beirut, Cairo, and Damascus, have been identified by Harkabi, op. cit., pp. 487–8. Only one is earlier than 1951. A further thirty-seven works published between 1947 and 1967, but mostly in the 1960s, either quote the *Protocols* extensively or else explicitly rely on them. Some of these works were issued by official bodies, including the Jordan Ministry of Education.

[12] Not merely in statements of policy, but in constitutional instruments as

public dissent, and little that is private. There are large political and military organizations founded upon this view and a great deal of money changes hands in the interests of implementing it.[13] In a word, the conflict with Israel has been thoroughly institutionalized on an ideology-intensive basis. There are thus strong grounds for believing that a genuine[14] resolution of the conflict on any terms other than those now predicated on all sides about its nature would amount to a political catastrophe for almost the entire gamut of the military and civil leadership, and first and foremost the leaders of the militant Palestinians themselves.

(4) The Jewish side is placed very differently. Both the situation of Israel and its 'case' require and rest on a preference for the *status quo* over all other conceivable situations—with many of the considerable political and psychological handicaps that tend to accrue in such instances.

The cardinal tenet of Zionism has long been fulfilled: the Jewish state has been re-established in the historic fatherland of the Jewish people. The great majority of Jewish communities in distress—all those, in fact, for whom Zionism constituted a practical as well as an ideologically attractive, or at any rate meaningful, solution to their problem (with the one great exception of Russian Jewry)—have been taken in and settled. Over forty-three per cent of the Jewish population of Israel is now native born and the proportion of native born is, of course, rising all the time.[15] In brief, Zionism as originally conceived has ceased to be an issue, except for individual *non*-Israelis, and that chiefly in the very narrow and marginal context of the opportunities Israel provides the Jew to identify himself fully and unreservedly with an ancestral culture should he wish to do so.

It is on practical and instrumental issues of public, social, economic, and foreign policy, not those of ideology, justice in the abstract, and on the nature of their enemies that the attention of Israel's

---

well. For example, Article 10 of the National Charter of the United Arab Republic (Egypt) provides for the liquidation of Israel—described as 'a dangerous pocket of imperialist resistance to the peoples' struggle'.

[13] According to a Kuwait Government source (28 December 1969) $156 million, or a quarter of the Kuwait budget is allocated for assistance to Egypt and Jordan. The guerrilla organizations would be getting $57 million in the same year. All told, according to the same source, Kuwait, Saudi, and Libyan contributions to the war against Israel would amount to $ 420 million.

[14] As opposed, for example, to a temporary concession designed to lever Israel out of its current (1971) military advantage and not intended to endure.

[15] 1967 figures: no less than eighty-eight per cent of Jewish children up to the age of fourteen are native born. It may also be worth noting that sixteen per cent of the native born are of native parentage and a further forty-six per cent of African and Asian parentage.

policy-makers and public alike is riveted. Indeed, were it not for the military threat which the Arabs pose the state and its citizens, Arab opposition to them would by and large be ignored, or at the very least treated as an unpleasant irritant or embarrassment to which some adjustment must reluctantly be made.

The fact is, of course, that the military pressure and threats have consistently been substantial, and have taken a great variety of forms all the way from primitive, pogrom-like attacks on Jewish communities in the 1920s to repeated attempts to wage both total, technically sophisticated war, and systematic irregular warfare from 1948 onwards. This fairly persistent employment of armed violence against the *Yishuv* (or Jewish community in Palestine) and Israel has in time amounted to the key mode whereby the Arabs have made a psychological impact on the Jews; and it is therefore by these means above all that the Arabs have contributed to the essential framework of ideas within which the Jews interpret the conflict and set ways and means of coping with it. As Arab pressure has mounted in recent years and as Israelis can no longer ascribe to the Arab opponent any operational goal other than the physical liquidation of Israel along with the majority of its inhabitants, their approach to the conflict in its totality has been steadily pared of all base-lines and criteria beyond an ever more simple (if not simplistic) pragmatism.

One consequence of this approach to the opponent is that there has been nothing in Israel remotely like the massive political and institutional commitment to the conflict—still less to its perpetuation in the present form—that is to be observed on the Arab side. No leaders are bound to it. There are no organizations whose *raison d'être* is rooted in it. Those nationalist ideologues who do argue the historic and legal rights of the Jews to all of the former British mandated territories of Palestine and Transjordan have never made the slightest material effort to effect those rights since the state was established a generation ago; and today the nub of the argument they address to all but the initiated is essentially instrumental: security is best ensured by hanging on to the territories occupied in 1967. The armed forces themselves are, as is well known, composed preponderantly of reservist officers and men; furthermore, as the events of 1967 amply demonstrated, military leaders have only the barest influence on major policy (as opposed to tactical military) decisions. All in all, it is entirely typical that in the difficult period following the 1967 war, when military service and military expenditure have had to be greatly extended, both official policy and popular attitudes have been directed towards maintaining economic and social life on a level as close to the normal and the socially desirable as possible.

Another, politically much more important, consequence of this well-nigh exclusive preoccupation with what is and what is not conducive to social and physical survival is the inability of the Israel policy-making machinery to operate efficaciously in any but critical situations, indeed in any but the extreme situation of impending war. The origins of this weakness are partly institutional and partly conceptual. As already suggested, there is no significant dissent on what, for Jewish purposes, is the key issue of the conflict: survival. Disagreement (and hence dissent) occurs on the instrumental level and involves argument about which policies are best calculated to strengthen Israel's capabilities as opposed to weakening them. Since there can never be any simple and unequivocal answer to this kind of question except in purely military terms, and since Israel is an open society and is governed according to parliamentary rules—and the rules of proportional representation at that—policy-making tends to be reduced to, or even replaced by, a search for the lowest common denominator of the ruling party coalition. The propensity to settle for a combination of defensive military activism and diplomatic immobility, or, at the very least, to eschew political initiatives, is thus very great. It is certainly in marked contrast to the Arab posture which is founded on a narrow, but very specific and therefore operationally superior principle of action: the integration of Israel/ Palestine into the Arab sphere.

It remains to discuss the parties to the conflict at this latter, operational level.

(5) It was suggested that the parties to the conflict can be seen as comprising two great, geographically widespread, somewhat unsteady and, in some important respects, heterogeneous coalitions. In each case, the differences and contradictions within each group tend to be offset in one degree or another by powerful, but again unequal and unsteady, ties of identity. The identification of the circumstances in which the common ties will operate—or can be made to operate— most powerfully is therefore crucial to an assessment of how the coalitions may be expected to act against each other, above all in crisis.

The short answer to this question is that the Arab coalition holds together best in the long term, while the Jewish coalition is only fully effective at the brink of impending catastrophe. This would appear to follow quite naturally both from the differing situations in which each is placed and from the views of the conflict which predominate on each side. As the Arab coalition is almost identical with the states members of the Arab League, it is able to function authoritatively through the machinery of the governments concerned.

Moreover, as indicated, there are ample political constraints against deviation. So long as the costs of involvement in the conflict are relatively small, or thought to be small (as they were thought to be even on the eve of war in 1967), the coalition is capable of acting with a marked degree of unity. It will be particularly effective in the international diplomatic context where the emphasis is necessarily on a common verbal front. But it will be capable of co-operation and co-ordination on the military plane as well. It is when the anticipated and assessed costs of involvement begin to rise too rapidly that the effectiveness of the coalition is in doubt. The more concrete the issues and the greater their consequent amenability to hard assessment, the greater will be the general propensity to take stock and reconsider where particularist interests lie. Where military defeat clearly threatens or, say, the loss of oil revenues, or the loss of territory, or a serious weakening of the regime, there will invariably be some fading out from the operative coalition and a reduction in its effective membership, at any rate where such fading out is possible. For it is not always possible. The weaker the regime, for example, the less it can withstand nationalist pressure to remain in the van against Israel. Where high material and political costs have already been suffered—as by Jordan and Egypt after the June war— the broad anti-Israel drive will, on the contrary, be reinforced by the specific (and particularist) political and emotional need to restore the *status quo ante*.

The logic of these familiar dilemmas requires the Arab side, if it is to hold together in crisis at approximately the level of its nominal membership, to seek to build up the greatest possible military establishment and, simultaneously, to subject Israel to whatever pressures seem likely to sap the latter's strength. In this way the Arabs may hope to reduce the costs of ultimate confrontation to an acceptable minimum and open the way to achievement of the common goal. For if they cannot act in concert they cannot really act at all—at all events, not without the active support of an external power as surrogate for the absent members of the Arab coalition.

The Jewish coalition presents a very different aspect. Jews in Israel and Jews elsewhere live under different political authorities and the ability of the Israel government to lead the Diaspora is limited in kind to a measure of vague moral pressure and limited in extent to the conscious adepts of the Israel cause. Beyond the latter lies the broad band of individual Jews who go about their business with very little thought to these questions, apart from an occasional twinge of sympathy when events in the Middle East are prominently reported in the mass media. And beyond these again is the much narrower band of the totally unengaged. In what exact proportions the various Jewish communities actually divide into adepts, sympathizers, and the entirely indifferent or even hostile, it is quite impossible to assess. But there is the evidence of Jewish behaviour in May 1967—before the June war, when the worst was feared—to indicate that support and sympathy are at their widest and deepest, which is to say, the Jewish coalition tends to be at its highest operational level, at precisely those times when the Arab coalition is itself at its most coherent, effective, and promising. So if to this is added the fact noted earlier that Israel policy-makers are at *their* most effective in crisis, it will be seen that the closer the Arab coalition approaches, or is thought by either side to approach, its goal, the more it tends to strengthen and unite its opponent. At the same time, the nearer the crisis, and the more closely Jews in and outside Israel pull together, the more strongly are the Arabs confirmed in their unrelenting view of Israel and the firmer becomes their determination to destroy it. It is, perhaps, in this curious and possibly unique symbiotic relationship between the disputants that the main elements of the tragedy lie.

But this is not all. The duality of Arab interests encourages Israel to seek to deter pressure and disrupt the coalition by maximizing the actual or potential costs of conflict to the individual Arab states and organizations. Like the Arabs, Israel must therefore seek to build up as large and efficacious a military establishment as possible. But in fact, Israel's ability to deter the Arab coalition is very uncertain. Judged in the light of the first, quasi-objective level, of analysis suggested earlier, the Israel military potential cannot but seem small when set against the vast human and financial resources and great military build-up available to the Arabs. And the more powerful the members of the Arab coalition grow—and the more effectively the coalition may be expected to operate—the greater must the imbalance appear. Israel therefore attempts to deter not merely by amassing and parading its military capabilities, but by repeatedly demonstrating their effectiveness in the field. And when the level of arms on the opposing side appears to be rising too fast relative to that of Israel's, the balance of advantage for Israel will always lie in pre-emptive war. But here again, each one of Israel's military successes, each attempt to deter or disrupt or incapacitate the coalition, serves equally to confirm and intensify the Arab tendency, however unsteady, to act in unison and to see in Israel a threat to the pan-Arab cause as a whole, and in its very presence in the Levant a painful and open wound in the Arab body politic. Finally, that military encounters should occur against a background of repeated insistence by Israel that it wishes for no more than peace and security, is generally held on the Arab side to constitute so much additional evidence of Israel's essential perfidy and malevolence. For their part, the Arabs can argue that they, at any rate, never have, and do not now, proclaim their aims to be peace and coexistence. To which the ever more conscious and explicit response of the Israelis is to discount the expectation of an eventual resolution of the conflict in terms of peace and security for all, and to accept a prospect of interminable minor warfare punctuated from time to time by major clashes.

Each side is thus either committed or constrained to see in the other an opponent to be confronted by nothing less than unremitting hostility. The goals are in each case such that the closer they are to attainment the more strongly the parties are impelled to pursue them. In these circumstances it is not surprising that the chronology of the Arab–Israel conflict should be one of spiralling violence. Nor, for all these reasons, is it possible to envisage a radical change in the structure of the conflict, still less in its climate, without prior and equally radical change in the identity and goals of the parties to it.

In practice, such a change could only occur in the wake of one or more of the following: the abandonment of pan-Arabism, i.e. the concept of the common interests and identity of all Arabs; the establishment of Israel's military security on so firm a basis that the realization of Arab goals would manifestly have to be postponed to the Greek calends; the successful liquidation of Israel and the death and dispersal of its Jewish inhabitants; or the successful imposition of a settlement by the great powers. Of none of these four possibilities is there today much prospect; but each may be very briefly considered.

An attempt has already been made to indicate how profound are the roots of the pan-Arab ideology in the contemporary Arab world and why the conflict between Arabs and Jews is far from being a mere territorial dispute between the two major ethnic groups which inhabit 'Palestine'. The position is that any concession to the Jewish national movement, any measure of acquiescence in the perpetuation of a Jewish state of any dimension whatsoever, is held to be a betrayal of a constituent member of the family of Arab peoples, the Palestinians. Accordingly, the settlement which from the Jewish point of view is least desirable, but still conceivably acceptable—a fresh partition of Palestine—would still entail either the abandonment of the Palestinians by the other Arabs or else a resolve by the Palestinians to make their own peace with the Jews and stand alone.

Neither possibility is in prospect. No Arab government would dare undertake the former and few have any real need to; and such feeble attempts by moderate Palestinians to negotiate independently with

Israel as occurred after the end of the Six Days War rapidly withered. They neither wished nor dared to cut themselves off from their neighbours in so unpopular a cause and they have never been influential enough even in their own areas to make it worth Israel's while to negotiate with them. In the meantime the hard-line Palestine Liberation Organization, which comprises about a dozen of the principal guerrilla organizations, and the still more intransigent groups led by Georges Habash and Naif Hawatmeh, all of which are fully in key with the conventional Arab approach to the problem, are taking most of the initiatives. So while the freeing of the Palestinians from the tutelage of the other Arabs opened up the possibility of a direct settlement between them and the Jews *in theory*, in practice the dominant Palestinian parties are pressing the other way.

The three remaining possibilities all involve the powers that are external to the region—first and foremost the United States and the Soviet Union. Israel's human and material resources are too limited for it to establish itself in Arab minds as invulnerable. So, short of a still unimaginably profound breakthrough in military technology, it is hard to see how the Arab world could be persuaded to give up the struggle, unless a lasting and credible military link were established between Israel and one of the primary powers. On the other hand, the Arab states, for all their incomparably greater military potential, are unlikely to achieve the straightforward victory over Israel to which they are committed unless they are aided by one of the powers in ways that go substantially beyond the forms of assistance (supplies, intelligence, technical advisers, and operational assistance limited to aircraft and missile troops) with which the Soviet Union provides them at present.[16]

Neither of these two possibilities is inconceivable and the latter (increased Soviet aid) as things stand at the time of writing, is marginally more likely than the former (alignment of Israel with the US). Yet neither is really easy to envisage, as the discussion of the inter-relation between small and great power politics in the Middle East in the second half of this chapter will show. The essential and general point to be made at this stage is that the structure and dynamic of the Arab–Israel conflict owe almost nothing of real substance to external factors. In all significant respects it constitutes a system, the parts of which are able and willing to draw upon the political and material resources of the extra-regional powers only to the extent that the latter can serve the regional powers' own, internal purposes. Thus while the conflict attained its mature phase well over two decades ago and has persisted in broadly identical form ever

[16] July 1971.

since, all of the primary powers have thought it politic to change sides at least once.[17]

The last of the four ways in which the conflict might terminate is inherently the least likely. The primary powers can probably enforce a temporary cessation of hostilities for a while. They may even succeed—although this is more doubtful—in imposing a territorial settlement of their own devising. But the motor forces driving the Arab and Jewish national movements are so powerful and the attachment of each side to its respective position so fervent, that no imposed settlement could be expected to endure very long: a large and fully viable Israel would continue to serve as a goad to Arab revanchism; a moderately reduced Israel would encourage the Arabs to persevere; a greatly reduced Israel would encourage the Arabs and impel the Jews to reverse the process. And so unless the primary powers were prepared to impose full control over the region in forms that might well be reminiscent of classic nineteenth-century imperialism it would not be too long before the *status quo ante* was restored.

Russians and Americans

(1) For over fifteen years the active, thrusting extra-regional power in the Middle East has been the Soviet Union. The other extra-regional powers which played or still play a role of consequence—Britain and France at the beginning of the period, but now the United States virtually alone—constitute, to adapt Clausewitz's phrase, part of the resistant medium through which the Russians move. It is the difference between an aggressive strategy and a defensive one; and it is crucial.

A discussion of the role the primary powers play in the conflict and, contrariwise, the role the conflict plays in the calculations and policies of the primary powers, must therefore centre on the moves made and the directions taken by the Soviet Union; and it must consider the United States more in terms of the broad pattern of its reactions to these moves, than in its own right.

The sources and goals of Soviet foreign policy in that part of the Middle East in which the Arab–Israel conflict is being played out are

[17] The Soviet Union favoured the establishment of Israel and supported it against the Arabs. Britain strongly supported the Arabs. The United States opposed the establishment of the state and only reversed its position after the Israelis defied Secretary Marshall's dire warnings and presented the Americans with the prospect of a *fait accompli*. Nevertheless, even after the formal point had been conceded, a severe embargo on arms was maintained. As the Arabs were well provided with (British) arms, the effect of the American embargo was even more serious than the better known one imposed by the French twenty years later. The bulk of Israel's arms duly came from the Soviet side.

F

not a little obscure—more so than elsewhere, if only because of the Russians' long absence from the region. It is nevertheless possible to argue that successive bursts of Russian activity in the Middle East over the past three decades or so have coincided with one or more of the following developments: an attempt by other rival extra-regional powers to penetrate the area; the impending collapse of an established preponderant power and the prospect of an ensuing period of uncertainty which another major power might well exploit; and the prospect of an independent exploitation of Middle East contingencies and opportunities in the interests of furthering Soviet goals elsewhere. Only very recently has evidence accumulated which points to a factor which is of intrinsic value in Soviet eyes, namely oil.[18] For the rest, it is a reasonably safe assumption that it is essentially as a marginal increment to the total array of the Soviet Union's political and strategic assets, not excluding the intangibles of prestige and status as the anointed rival of the United States for world leadership, that the Middle East figures in the eyes of that country's masters. It is in this light that Soviet initiatives since the end of the Second World War are probably best understood, among them one of the most curious and important of all: the support in the form of military supplies and political backing which was given Israel at its birth.

It is worth noting, in this connection, that Stalin was warned by foreign affairs subordinates not to support the Jews and not to recognize Israel lest the policy reversal disqualify all subsequent attempts to make common cause with the Arabs. His response was that in ten years time the Arabs would have forgotten or have abandoned their conflict with the Jews; and if not, there would still be ample time to think again.[19] Stalin was aware of the catastrophe that had befallen European Jewry and there is no question that he understood, and to some extent expected to capitalize upon, Jewish national sentiments. But of greater importance was the fact that Stalin was still intent in 1947 and 1948, as he had been from 1943 onwards, on replacing Britain as the second of the world powers and establishing, conjointly with the United States, a new world order based on what in modern terminology would be termed a bi-polar international system. In the context of the times, support for the Jewish *Yishuv* meant a blow at Britain and her Arab client

---

[18] Soviet oil requirements are increasing faster than expected domestic production; moreover, the exhaustion of oil wells west of the Urals will force the use of distant eastern fields at high cost in transport. Import of Middle East oil at about half the unit price would be economically advantageous and help slow down the depletion of domestic reserves. See Jean-Jacques Berreby, 'Growing Oil Needs Influence Soviet Policy', *The New Middle East*, December 1969.

[19] Private source.

states above all else. And it might be expected to have two promising by-products: an alignment with the United States on an issue about which substantial sections of American public opinion (primarily, but not exclusively, Jewish) felt strongly, even though the President's advisers, like those of Stalin, were powerfully opposed to what came to be settled policy; and secondly, the establishment of a new and promising foot-hold for the Russians themselves in a region from which they had been absent since the outbreak of the First World War. It is instructive, that by the early 1950s, when Stalin had become seriously concerned lest a new world war break out, Israel had already entered into Soviet contingency planning as a potential 'popular democracy' to be taken over by the left-wing elements in its population who would then, in turn, provide the Soviet forces destined to thrust down into the Near East through Turkey and Syria (simultaneously with a massive invasion of Western Europe) with a welcome *point d'appui*.[20]

Nevertheless, for all the energy and great resources which the Soviet leaders have applied to their Middle East ventures in recent years and for all their often brilliant opportunism and seemingly disproportionate risk-taking, it would be a mistake to see them as embarked on a straightforward exercise in crass imperialism on the old turn-of-the-century model. The end result may not be very different, but the sources and mechanism are unique.

The vigorous and uninhibited pursuit of the tactical goals which the Soviet leadership sets itself from time to time seems to stem chiefly from their unremitting alertness to prospects for enhancing the security of both the Russian state and the political machinery by which they themselves run it, and from a parallel and extreme sensitivity to any possible threat to one or the other. Whether one chooses to see Soviet Russia as an unwieldy and unfortunate giant perpetually thrashing about in an effort to defend itself from both real and imagined attack, or, instead, as a monster bent assiduously on aggression, is thus almost a question of taste. What matters in practice is that the profound lack of ease and self-confidence with which the Soviet leaders (and the leaders of Imperial Russia before them) contemplate the world, impels them to seek to establish a sort of *cordon sanitaire* in reverse around the borders of their state.

Broadly speaking, the interest taken by the Soviet Union in the Middle East states *immediately* adjoining their territory, Turkey and Iran, is very similar to its interest in the states of the Baltic and the Balkans and, of course, in the Central European states which lie between. Where a working arrangement on the basis of Soviet confidence in the tertiary state's neutrality has been possible, as

[20] Private source.

with Finland and, intermittently, with Turkey, a lack of direct control over its affairs may just be tolerable. But where there is manifestly no confidence in the future course of the state in question, every attempt will be made to bring it into line. And where, as in Eastern Europe, doubts were very great and the accidents of military occupation and the existence of some sort of indigenous communist movement facilitated a total take-over, the opportunity was seized without inhibition and no subsequent escape from the Soviet-controlled system allowed. On the other hand, where that extra-regional primary power which is seen as the potential or actual source of pressure on the Soviet Union has clearly asserted its will and shown its ability to protect the buffer state, the Russians have invariably accepted the resultant line of demarcation, at any rate *de facto*.

What appears to be difficult for the Soviet leaders to live with is a situation intermediate between total control (or at least a form of guaranteed neutrality on the Finnish model)[21] and a firm line of demarcation maintained by the rival primary power. Moreover, where they have succeeded in establishing unquestioned control—as in Eastern Europe—their obsession with total security will impel them to regard the buffer areas as so many new interests to protect. They will then seek to establish a new chain of buffer territories on which to found the security of the first. But again, where the new target of penetration and expansion is clearly and firmly proclaimed to be (or believed by the Russians to be) a subject of the other extra-regional power's interest, the effort will be relaxed as unreasonable and counter-productive.

Stalin turned to the uprising in Greece: 'The uprising in Greece will have to fold up.' (He used for this the word *svernut'*, which means literally *to roll up*.) 'Do you believe'—he turned to Kardelj—'in the success of the uprising in Greece?'

Kardelj replied, 'If foreign intervention does not grow, and if serious political and military errors are not made'.

Stalin went on, without paying attention to Kardelj's opinion: 'If, if! No, they have no prospect of success at all. What, do you think that Great Britain and the United States—the United States, the most powerful state in the world—will permit you to break their line of communication in the Mediterranean? Nonsense. And we have no navy. The uprising in Greece must be stopped, and as quickly as possible.'[22]

Smaller and weaker men than Stalin operating as an uneasy and suspicious collective cannot be expected to be capable of making such harsh reversals of policy as did Stalin himself. But their fear of change and of the consequences of a loss of control over what they

[21] Discussed in detail as the third paradigm in Chapter Four below.
[22] Milovan Djilas, *Conversations with Stalin*, London, 1962, p. 164.

have come to regard as theirs will, if anything, be greater, as the 1968 invasion of Czechoslovakia showed so clearly.

In sum, Soviet policy in the Middle East at its most basic is a part product of the persistent quest for what might be termed absolute security. It is modified by, and in a sense founded on, a concomitant disposition to accept that the rival power or powers will be driven—by a different order of causes and motives, no doubt, but with much the same results—to take up the slack in the opposite direction. And with this goes a corresponding readiness to make an agreed division into spheres of primary power influence provided the line of demarcation is reasonably clear and the other side's will to maintain it is beyond doubt—as with the Germans in 1939 and with the Americans in Europe in 1945–8. It is when there is doubt about the other side's firmness (as in the case of Khrushchev and Kennedy at their Vienna meeting in 1961) that the offensive–defensive strategy of the Soviet Union leads to a crossing of the nominal boundaries of the spheres of interest—as occurred in the Berlin crisis of that year and the Cuba missile crisis of the following year. So while the drive outwards to establish the absolute security of the Soviet state and of its political machine leads, in practice, to a form of continual pressure against all states which are judged actually or potentially hostile, or capable of disturbing the delicate balance of fear, loyalty, and mute acquiescence on which the Soviet state machine rests, it remains entirely within the power of Russia's rivals to circumscribe and offset it by applying countervailing pressure. On the other hand, once the Russians have established a military or political position and in so doing added to the bulwarks of their state and system, or simply to their capacity to launch further forays and probes into hostile territory by way of keeping the existing bulwarks in good order, it is both psychologically and politically difficult for them to retreat from it and they will do so only under the greatest possible pressure, as from Cuba in 1962. And even that retreat was no more than partial and the Cuban investment is still kept going at great expense and inconvenience. Moreover, it was a retreat for which Khrushchev was never forgiven and to which, in part, he probably owes his deposition. In short, successful Soviet advances tend, at the limit, to be irreversible.

(2) Seen in this light, the catalogue of Soviet achievements in the Middle East since the great return in 1955 is long and impressive. Partly through their own efforts, partly through vigorous exploitation of the loss of energy, self-confidence, and purpose in the West, but above all by offering themselves as *alternative* patrons to revolutionary regimes for whom disconnection from the West was the most

natural and essential symbol of change, and by adopting Arab causes
as their own, they have replaced the Western powers in Cairo,
Damascus, Baghdad, Tripoli, Khartoum, Algiers, Sa'ana, and Aden,
as the prime political partner and protector. They supply and train
all major Arab armies. They are the indispensable diplomatic pro-
moters of Arab causes in the United Nations. It is to them that the
major Arab calls for economic aid are now addressed. And, in
exchange, the Russians have seen all Western military bases elimi-
nated from these countries along with any reasonable prospect of the
Arab states being recruited for Western political causes, even such
minor, verbal ones as joint public condemnation of the Soviet
invasion of Czechoslovakia in 1968. Finally there is the new naval
presence in the Mediterranean, the Persian Gulf, and the Indian
Ocean, relying upon a string of permanent docking and supply
facilities in Arab ports which are bases in all but name (an important
formal distinction, but no more) to serve as a tangible expression of
Russia's new and widespread extra-territorial military and political
capabilities in the region. Soviet naval forces have been brought into
permanent station off the straits of Gibraltar and the Tyrrhenian
Sea and their passage through the Aegean and the Malta Channel is
a matter of routine. The ancient Russian drive towards the warm
waters to the south and west of its home territory has thus achieved
dramatic expression.

The ultimate implications of the development are still far from
clear. What *is* evident is that this great expansion of extra-territorial
military capability is able to serve the long-established Soviet belief
in, and desire for, instruments of policy which are entirely subject to
their will. Economic and cultural penetration is too uncertain. KGB-
manipulated agents of influence may be easily identified and removed by opponents. Only the military arm and ultimately, of
course, the KGB in its uniformed and armed manifestations are
wholly satisfactory. And it is only the firm wielding of much the
same, fully controllable and malleable instruments of power by their
opponents that convinces them of their opponents' reality and
ensures that their hostility is noted and enters into the Russians' own
calculations.

Broadly, the uses to which the new Red Fleet in the Mediterranean
may plausibly be put would seem to fall into two inter-connected
categories: the first might crudely be called psychological; the other
pertains to the strategic sphere proper. Into the mental or psychological category fall all those activities which serve to assist Russian
policy without necessarily involving the firing of so much as a
signal flare. They range from what the Victorians called 'showing
the flag'—i.e. making an impression on the impressionable—

to the more modern and infinitely more complex matter of ensuring that they, the Russians, enter into the calculations of the other side and inhibit it accordingly.[23] An American decision to repeat the kind of operation that was mounted in Lebanon in 1958 would now have to take the Russians into account and would either not be made at all, or would be made after greater hesitation and in a much warier and less determined spirit. This result, a direct consequence of the Russian naval presence in the Mediterranean, is in itself no small gain.

But the strictly strategic implications of the Russian entry into the Mediterranean are much more serious. First and foremost the Russians are now well equipped to employ the American tactic of instituting a 'quarantine', i.e. an interdictory blockade against any of the littoral states. Any move to break such a blockade would imply armed conflict with the Soviet Union—or might be thought to do so. And indeed, the institution of such a blockade would be, in effect, a message to all concerned that the Soviet Union was prepared to enter into conflict.

Henceforth, a state subjected to Soviet blockade—for whatever reason—can resist compulsion only if its leaders' nerves are stronger than those of the Russians, or if the United States backs it. But American support would depend on Washington's willingness to become even more dangerously involved in the affairs of the littoral states than it is already. And the very presence of the Red Fleet in the Mediterranean may accelerate the American disposition to disengage and limit their commitments, rather than the reverse.

The other major implications of the Soviet build-up is that it provides a new instrument of military pressure and incursion against a whole new range of states which have neither formal guarantees of American protection through NATO or CENTO, nor nuclear weapons of their own. Whereas in northern Europe all states have already been compelled to opt either for armed neutrality or inclusion in one or other of the military alliance systems (Finland being a very special case, but nevertheless firmly within the Soviet orbit from the military aspect), Spain, North Africa, and much of the Middle East (all of the Middle East, if the Canal opens) are for the first time facing some very hard choices.

Unlike the situation obtaining when Prague was first taken over by

[23] According to an unconfirmed but undenied newspaper report (*Ha'aretz*, 9 February 1970) the Soviet government drew the attention of the Israel government in the summer of 1969 to the presence of Russian warships on permanent station at Port Said and to the danger to which Israel's military activity in the area was subjecting them. The message is said to have been transmitted through the Finnish Embassy in Tel Aviv.

the Soviet Union (1948), there is no evidence that the Americans are prepared to extend their nuclear umbrella over additional candidates. Moreover, their doctrine of flexible response casts doubts on the value of that umbrella.

In this respect those states which have resolved on the fullest possible Soviet orientation are probably the worst placed of all. They cannot hope for American support against the Russians until they themselves have moved against them. Yet any such move against the Russians by, say, the Syrians, or the Egyptians, or the Algerians, in the not impossible eventuality of a change of heart or regime, would now strike at the heart of a working, major Soviet politico-military interest—the Red Mediterranean Fleet itself—and the Americans would correspondingly be as disinclined to quarrel with the Russians about it as the Russians were to quarrel with them in the Caribbean.

All in all then, the post-Stalin Middle East policy of the Soviet Union has been extremely profitable in two great inter-connected fields: national security capabilities and the East–West balance of forces and influence. Moreover, it has provided an important and, as may be supposed, particularly satisfying by-product: a reinforcement of the Soviet Union's status as a world power. The West is now anxious to accept the Russians as equal and necessary partners in the elaboration and imposition of a new order in the Middle East, and in a final settlement of the Arab–Israel conflict. Even a decade ago the thought of admitting the Soviet Union to the Concert of Powers for Middle East purposes was anathema in Washington. Now Washington has no choice in the matter.

But against the advantages to the Russians must be set the costs and the uncertainties. There are the vast economic costs of civil and military aid to the Arab states—an estimated $5,000–6,000 million in arms supplies alone since 1955. There are the political uncertainties and the risk of military encounter entailed in what is, among other things, a campaign to hasten the departure of Western European and American influence from 'regions near the frontiers of the U.S.S.R.' (as the area tends to be referred to in official statements of position). And there is the fundamental uncertainty about the Arabs themselves and the Soviet relationship with them.

Soviet success in the Middle East has been founded on an informal but none the less tight alliance with the Arabs; and the matter on which co-operation and alignment have been closest has been the issue of Israel. In the short-term, the advantages to both sides have been considerable: for the Arabs—economic aid, great quantities of modern arms, and well-nigh unlimited political support extending to a readiness to keep other outside powers from intervening whenever a political, or even a military,[24] defeat for Israel is in prospect; and for the Russians—the very possibility of implementing the policy lines already discussed. But in the long-term, the ability of the Russians to maintain and secure the positions and advantages gained so dramatically since the first arms deal was negotiated through the Czechs in February 1955 hinges on continuing Arab dependence. And this, in turn, hinges upon three questions. First, is the extension of Soviet influence in the Middle East, and in the Levant in particular, truly irreversible, which is to say, will the Soviet presence ultimately take on a more concretely neo-imperialist form such that the Arabs would not be *allowed* to break their ties with Russia should they desire to do so?

For the present, the Russians have no evident incentive to attempt to reinforce a successful alliance by methods which might endanger its continuance in the short-term and impel some Arabs to have second thoughts about the retreat of the West from the eastern Mediterranean. But ultimately, as the Western retreat continues and as the Russians' positions become increasingly familiar and established and tend, moreover, to be recognized internationally, the south-eastern Mediterranean basin may come to be viewed as a sort of Soviet-dominated Caribbean—perhaps with Israel as the Western Cuba. It is not totally improbable that, by the end of the 1970s, a Soviet action to restore order in the Arab ranks would be met with the kind of verbal disapproval covering implicit acquiescence that constituted the net international reaction to the American intervention in Guatemala in 1954 and the Dominican Republic in 1965.

For the time being, however, Arab dependence on the Soviet Union is likely to turn more significantly upon a second question, namely whether the groups—chiefly of military origin and relying on regular armed forces as the base of their power—which now rule most Arab states, including all those which maintain close ties with the Russians, will continue to see their own political destinies as being linked to the Russian alliance. From their point of view, there will be the danger that a reversal of alliances would not only carry little or no advantage, either as regards the war with Israel or any other major issue, but would appear—or could be made to appear— a failure on which rival groups might capitalize. Moreover, just as it is not merely politically, but also doctrinally and psychologically

---

[24] It was not until late (New York time) on 6 June, when it was becoming clear that the Egyptians were about to be defeated that the Russians changed their line from one of keeping the Powers to the ringside to that of pressing heavily for a United Nations (i.e. Russo-American) imposed ceasefire on whatever terms they could get.

convenient for the Russians to link up with the dominant movement of ideas and political action in the Arab world today, so the Russian link is vastly more congenial, natural, and workable for the quasi-socialist and authoritarian pan-Arabists, than an alliance with the complex, sophisticated Western politics from under the heavy hand of which they feel they have barely emerged.

But it is on a third question, the state of the Arab–Israel conflict, that the future of Soviet–Arab relations is likely to turn before all else. This is not merely because the conflict provided the original major opening for the Russian penetration of the area, or even that it continues to provide the day-to-day meat of co-operation between the Soviet Union and its Arab clients. It is primarily because the continuing war with Israel fuels the pan-Arab movement and makes some sort of hegemonic structure possible in the Arab world. Were the Russians forced to deal with the fourteen disparate and rival states on an exclusively bilateral basis they would be drawn much deeper than they are already into the complexities of inter-Arab politics. Instead, like the British and the Americans before them, they have very reasonably preferred to deal with the major Arab states, with Egypt above all, both for their intrinsic importance and for the leadership they can provide on what might be called a sub-contracting basis. (The weakness of the American position in the Arab world at the time of writing is precisely because of their lack of an Arab partner that can serve as a really convincing candidate for hegemonic rank.) An ending of the conflict would entail the collapse, or, at the very least, a great weakening of the hegemonic structure and a re-opening of the region to other, rival, extra-regional powers at the behest of Arab governments seeking outside aid and comfort to further their particularist interests at the expense of their local adversaries. By the same token, the longer the Arab–Israel conflict endures, and the greater its hold over the sentiments and imagination of the Arab peoples, the more readily will the leadership of the states or movements which are Israel's effective opponents be accepted and the stronger becomes the position of the extra-regional power which is prepared to back the leading Arab state in the Arab national cause as compared with the extra-regional power which either hesitates or refuses to do so.

A smooth relationship along these lines between the Russians and the Arab hegemonic power is only liable to disturbance where the latter's hegemonic status is itself in question. In the present context, this means a situation where there is a manifest failure to pursue Arab goals in the conflict with Israel with either vigour or success. To restrain the state which must be in the van against Israel is therefore fatal not only to that state but also to Russia; and to join the

Americans in an attempt to impose a settlement which the Arab hegemonic power and its allies are not prepared to accept even tacitly is equally impossible. In this sense, the Russians are impelled to cleave to Arab policy lines in all but the most extreme situation, where a confrontation with the United States would be both certain and potentially painful—as the diplomatic history of the period before and after the Six Days War so clearly shows. When the hegemonic power fails to be in the van against Israel because it has a rival in the latter role, the problem is much more difficult.

The role of hegemonic power in the Arab world has been played traditionally and successfully by the strongest and most obvious candidate for it, Egypt. It is the most populous, the most prestigious, the most sophisticated, the most powerful militarily, and so placed geographically that it is a natural centre of the Arab world and also on the borders of Israel itself. None of the other candidates really match Egypt in any of these respects. Algeria, perhaps the closest in rank, is geographically too remote from the arena to be the champion of pan-Arabism, except as the recognized centre of expertise on the subject of guerrilla warfare. But the rise in the popularity of guerrilla warfare against Israel, if only as a means of easing Arab frustrations in the face of Israel's manifest ability to withstand conventional military attack for a long time to come, poses very great difficulties in this respect for Egypt and for Russia.

As a technique, guerrilla warfare has been vociferously adopted by the Palestinians and in so doing they have tended to wrest from the Egyptians some of the latter's long established primacy in the conflict. Moreover, the expulsion of the Egyptians from the Gaza Strip and from Sinai in 1967 automatically deprived them even of the possibility of exercising a kind of patronage over the Palestinians: the bases from which the latter must operate now lie in territory controlled, after a fashion, by the Syrians, the Jordanians, and the Lebanese, none of whom have reasons to regret the resultant diminution of Egyptian prestige. And from afar, the Palestinians have the moral and financial support of the Algerians, the Iraqis, the Saudis, and the Kuwaitis, all of whom have equal, if not greater, reason to embarrass Cairo. But, of course, from the Russian point of view the Palestinians are not even remote candidates for the subcontracting role which they have allotted Egypt, even if they were prepared to support them on other grounds. The Palestinians cannot aspire to regional hegemony, their methods and ideology put them closer to Peking than Moscow, and public backing of them would amount to wedding Russia almost irrevocably, certainly publicly, to the cause of liquidating Israel—which makes very little sense from the Russian point of view. The most significant and identifiable

Soviet purposes are served by the perpetuation of the Arab–Israel conflict at a high level of tension—for the sporadic, militarily unimpressive efforts of the Palestinians only begin to be significant as the temperature falls on the major Arab–Israel front between Israel and Egypt. It is only a lapse of the conflict into quiescence, to say nothing of its termination, that the Russians need fear.

The worst of all contingencies, from the Russian point of view, would be yet another defeat of the Arab forces by Israel, particularly if it led to a marked, even if temporary, slackening of the Arab will to regain Palestine and a tendency to turn to other affairs in the meantime. The impotent rage with which the Russians reacted to the Arab defeat in 1967 may be taken as an earnest of what might be expected in such an event. In fact, it is doubtful whether they could allow themselves to stand by and watch yet another group of Arab armies which they had trained and supplied destroyed in battle. The impulsion to intervene might be irresistible. Here, as elsewhere, the limits of Russian behaviour are set by the Americans, or by the Russian view of likely American behaviour.

In contrast, a minor military victory or major diplomatic victory for the Arabs would be welcomed, so long as Israel remained in being and continued to concentrate Arab attention upon it. Such a victory would encourage the Arabs to persevere and would, indirectly, redound to the credit of the Russians and also keep the alliance on its present course. A policy of this sort, designed to help the Arabs to inflict a less than fatal blow on Israel, seems to have been adopted in the period just before the June war and did a great deal to precipitate it. Nevertheless, the fact that the war ended in disaster would be less a reason for reverting to a more restrained form of support for Arab purposes, than for pursuing the same course more carefully and more efficaciously in the future. On the other hand, a *major* defeat of Israel would be quite another matter. It would dissolve the cement which binds the Arab world together and which makes possible the strengthening of the Soviet positions in the Middle East as well as the maintenance of a working alliance with the major Arab states. If this cement were dissolved, the Russians would have to face the difficult problem of perpetuating their preponderance by other means, or run the risk of a gradual erosion of their newly established positions.

It follows that the Soviet attitude to the very idea of a settlement engineered and imposed by themselves and the Americans jointly, can only be ambivalent. On the one hand, the effect of such a settlement would be to consolidate and legitimize their newly acquired status as a Middle East power. It would have the added advantage of implying, and perhaps even formalizing, an enduring division of the eastern Mediterranean area into American and Russian spheres of influence. Finally, a Russo–American settlement, suitably dressed in United Nations robes, might hold some attraction as a *pis aller* and temporary respite for both the Arabs and the Russians, should the dangers of a new round of major fighting with Israel appear too great.

Nevertheless, the underlying significance of Russo–American co-operation (provided it were genuine) would be to alter the character of the Arab–Soviet alliance. From being backers of the pan-Arab cause, the Russians would turn into moderators. They would have to abandon their policy of almost unlimited verbal support ('Israel is following in the footsteps of the Hitlerite criminals'.)[25] and would be impelled to adopt a posture of restraint. Arab suspicions would begin to grow. Arab irritability, now kept under control, would erupt. The honeymoon would be over. So while the Soviet leaders have good reason to keep the American option open as long as they can, if possible indefinitely, there would have to be a radical change in the circumstances of the conflict before such an option would be willingly taken up.

These might be grounds for believing that, given the present circumstances and assuming no radical change in the general structure of the conflict, the Russo–Arab alliance can be maintained on existing lines for a very long time to come. But this is to pay insufficient attention to the internal dynamic of the conflict at its lower tier which, in its essentials, operates autonomously; for the Soviet Union can only exploit and to some extent participate in the conflict if it aligns itself with the Arab cause. As a result Israel finds itself, in effect, pitted against the Soviet Union and bound to attempt the frustration of *Soviet* purposes, no less than Arab. Unacceptable to the Arabs, the *status quo* which Israel seeks to maintain has thus come to be unacceptable to the Soviet Union. The longer it endures, the greater are the risks to the Arab governments and movements which have claimed to be in the van against Israel and, by extension, the greater are the risks to the Russians. For the success of Israel cuts cleanly between Arabs and Russians. It reveals the weakness of the Arabs and it demonstrates the limits of Russian aid and comfort. It tends to expose the Arabs to isolation precisely at the time of their greatest need. It also impels them to look beyond the Russian alliance —to the Chinese and, latterly, now that the British and the French have veered round and disengaged politically and militarily from Israel, to the lesser Western powers—for leverage *vis-à-vis* the Soviet Union. Israel's success continually forces the Russians to go beyond whatever limits they have set from time to time to their

[25] Soviet government statement, *Pravda*, 23 March 1968.

involvement and it repeatedly upsets the delicate balance between the policies pursued in the Middle East and their policies elsewhere.

It must therefore be supposed that the Soviet leaders are under a slowly increasing compulsion to consider whether the balance of advantages does not lie, after all, in more extensive and more direct intervention on the Arab side—somewhat along the pattern of the American involvement in Vietnam and for roughly similar reasons.[26] Yet whether the prospect of Soviet intervention would suffice to inhibit Israel from applying itself to the preservation of the *status quo* is doubtful: impending defeat at the hands of the Arabs would not be made more palatable to Israel by the fact that the Russians were accelerating it. If in the face of Israel's resistance they were to stop half way, as the Americans have in Vietnam, they would risk the same ignominy of failure that the United States has incurred and precisely that break with the Arabs that they wish to avoid. If they did not stop, they would risk having to pour ever greater resources into the conflict, again like the Americans, and see the conversion of a barely manageable situation into one that *might* be wholly un-manageable and have incalculably severe international repercussions.

No doubt, it is this latter consideration which is critical for the Russians and works backwards through their tactical moves in the Middle East from day to day. It can therefore be argued, once again, that the success of present Soviet policy and, above all, the degree to which the Soviet Union can finally establish itself in the Middle East in terms of both political depth and geographical extension depends, in limiting situations, on the purposes of the United States and the efforts it is prepared to make in pursuing them. It is the constraining structure of the conflict at both its tiers which limits the Soviet Union's freedom of action in its conflict with Israel and which, for that very reason, has made the conflict a tenable one for the Israelis —thus far.

(3) If the central purpose of the United States in the Middle East were to confuse and frustrate the Soviet Union it would not be too difficult to suggest, on the basis of the foregoing analysis, how that purpose might be furthered. The Russians are critically dependent on their working alliance with the leading Arab states and it is the continuing conflict between Arabs and Jews which makes that alliance both possible and desirable. Possible, because the Arab side looks to the Soviet Union for the aid which offers the Arabs their one realistic hope of achieving the demolition of Israel; desirable, be-cause the conflict, as the engine of modern pan-Arabism, makes

[26] The generally accepted estimate of current (1971) involvement is one of between 15,000 and 20,000 Soviet servicemen in Egypt.

feasible the indirect but orderly recruitment of the bulk of the Arab world to Russian causes. On the other hand, the *autonomous* structure of the Arab–Jewish conflict weds Israel to a policy which tends to set the Arabs back, frustrate the purposes of the leading Arab states, disrupt the pan-Arab movement and thus, ultimately, frustrate the Russians in the Middle East as well. Clearly, then, if no radical change in the ability of Israel to set the leading Arab states back occurs, the Russo–Arab alliance will begin to crack. Either the Arabs' failure will make them reconsider the value of the alliance or else the Russians themselves will tire. It would therefore seem to follow that if the United States government were prepared to deter the Russians from still heavier support of the Arabs, dropping the restraint with which Israel is backed politically and assisted materially in its periodic efforts to top up its economic and military reserves through foreign loans and the purchase of foreign arms, the alliance between Russians and Arabs could be put in doubt and the still shaky structure of Soviet influence in the area with it. But, of course, the problems (and opportunities) which the Arab–Israel conflict sets the United States are not capable of reduction to such simple terms; and, in point of fact, America never has pursued such a policy of straightforward containment of the Russians in the Middle East, still less one of direct confrontation with them, nor can it be expected to do so.

In the first place, a policy along such lines is virtually what Israel has long pressed the United States to adopt—a fact which is almost enough to damn it from the outset. The proposition highlights the heart of the American dilemma; for it would amount to a policy that, in a general sense, was anti-Arab in all but name. True, it might partly coincide with the purposes of those minor Arab states which covertly resist the leadership of the claimants to hegemonic influence in the Arab world. But this could neither be publicly admitted, nor capitalized upon at all widely, for no American government will admit to a policy aimed at dividing the Arab world.[27] To do so would be to run counter to the principle of Arab unity and, by violating the cardinal taboo of the contemporary Arab world, make the further evolution of Arab–American relations excessively painful. To put the point somewhat differently, since the United States is anxious to retain a working relationship with *some* Arab states, it must, in effect, strive to avoid a serious quarrel with any of them. But to fail to support the Arab cause in the Arab–Israel conflict or, at the very least, to fail to adopt a strictly, unmistakably, and undeviatingly neutral posture, *is* to be at cross-purposes with at

[27] See, for example, Secretary of State Rogers's address on the Middle East, Washington, 9 December 1969.

least some Arab states—in fact, with those of the greatest weight in
the context of inter-Arab politics. Indeed, most American diplomatic
and academic specialists in Middle East affairs have been acutely
conscious of the cost of a course of action which, from 1948 onwards,
has often tended towards absolute neutrality, but has rarely rested
there for very long. Instead, the United States has tended to veer
continuously and erratically between two limits: between neutrality
on the one hand and, on the other hand, the lowest possible level of
support for Israel commensurate with the dictates of American global
policy and with the extremely complex structure of its bilateral
relations with Israel. The hypothetical alternative of competing with
the Russians by means of a wholeheartedly anti-Israel or anti-Jewish
policy has never been seriously tried. It may be supposed that if it
had been tried when there was the greatest chance of success—in the
1950s—it was unlikely to have succeeded, for reasons, incidentally,
which have nothing to do with Israel or the pro-Israel lobby in the
United States. The anti-Western content of the pan-Arab movement
was fully as strong, at the time, as the anti-Israel content; and more
powerful American support for Egypt and Algeria would have
entailed an even more profound quarrel with Britain and France
than that which finally erupted in 1956. At all events, since the
conversion of the Levant from the Western preserve it appeared to
be in the very early 1950s into the great arena of conflict between
Russia and the United States that it has become, the bilateral
American–Arab relationship has been replaced by a triangular
Russian–American–Arab one and it has become a great deal more
difficult to separate out the strictly regional threads of American
interest from its global interests.

It might be said here, parenthetically, that, on the whole, the
effect of this development on the general character of American–
Jewish relations has been tonic. So long as these were largely founded
on domestic political and ideological considerations—a philanthropic
view of the plight of the Jewish people by some, a xenophobic and
anti-Semitic rejection of prospective Jewish immigration into the
United States by others, and so forth—it was relatively simple for
the official American establishment to attempt to wash its hands of
the Jewish connection, much as the British had tried to do. For
against philanthropy could be set the dictates of *raison d'état*;[28] and

---

[28] Early in 1944 officials of the US Treasury prepared a document entitled
*Report to the Secretary on the Acquiescence of this Government in the Murder of
the Jews*, in which was asserted, among other things, that State Department
officials 'have not only failed to use the governmental machinery at their disposal
to rescue Jews from Hitler, but have even gone so far as to use this governmental

purely domestic political calculation could generally be nullified by
invoking that of external relations. However, the establishment of
the State of Israel, ironically with the belated and somewhat hesitant
blessing of the United States, and the acquisition by Jews of
independent political and military instrumentalities, introduced
parallel calculations of *raison d'état* of a different and contrary order.[29]
A typical consequence has been the appearance of divided counsels
within the American administration, even among the institutions
and officials specializing in foreign affairs, with the divides tending to
be along the lines of professional interests and commitment. For
example, the State Department, indissolubly attached, like most weak
foreign ministries, to the maintenance of regular bilateral relations
with foreign states on as wide and cordial a basis as possible, was
strongly opposed to the sale of 'Hawk' anti-aircraft missiles to Israel
in 1963. In contrast, the Defence Department, tending to see affairs
principally in cross-country terms and to concern itself with such
broad problems as the evolution of the total array of anti-Soviet
forces, was as strongly in favour of the sale of the 'Hawk'. Similarly,
at the height of the May/June crisis in 1967 the Pentagon appears to
have seen no obstacle to Israel's taking independent military action,
much to the embarrassment of both the Arabs and the Russians,
and incidentally letting the United States off the hook of its undertaking to keep the Straits of Tiran open to all shipping. Certainly,
the very last thing the Defence Department wished to risk in 1967
was a fresh overseas involvement of United States forces—a second
'Vietnam'. The State Department's position was entirely different.
It had literally forgotten the 1957 understanding into which the
United States had entered with Israel and which formed the basis on
which Israel was finally persuaded to hand over Sharm el-Sheikh to
the United Nations. This undertaking was that in the event of a
fresh blocking of the Straits of Tiran Israel would be entitled to re-
open them on its own account under Article 51 of the UN Charter
(the right of self-defence). The State Department thus saw no moral
or legal obstacle, still less political, to putting up opposition to
independent action by Israel and its first and characteristic reaction
to the outbreak of war was that 'our position is neutral in thought,
word and deed'.[30] True, in the face of the subsequent public and
congressional outcry, not to mention divided counsels within the
State Department itself, the official position was later softened to

machinery to prevent the rescue of these Jews'. Arthur D. Morse, *While Six
Million Died*, New York, 1968, p. 77.
[29] Which were more or less anticipated at the time.
[30] State Department spokesman, 5 June 1967.

G

'non-belligerence'. But the original formulation may be seen as representing some kind of ideal to which American diplomats have repeatedly attempted to adhere.

In sum, while the pursuit of policies hostile to the Soviet Union and cool or lukewarm to Israel may be just barely compatible with the maintenance of a form of political influence (and the safeguarding of economic interests) in the so-called conservative Arab states, such policies are wholly incompatible with genuine political co-operation with the 'radical' states. However, for that very reason, the pursuit of such policies tends, in the long term, to make the inter-Arab position of those states which *have* remained friendly to the United States extremely difficult and, perhaps, ultimately untenable. For on the pan-Arab level of action and argument it puts such states out of court, unless of course they join the pan-Arab movement, at least to the extent of participation in the conflict with Israel. The United States thus finds itself in an extraordinary predicament. It must either tolerate a direct strengthening of the anti-Israel forces and an indirect reinforcement of the pro-Russian group by its own remaining political partners in the Arab world; or else risk the washing away of its residual political and economic positions in the area.

Faced with these dilemmas the United States appears to have the choice of two broad policy options. It can attempt to preserve the autonomy of those Arab states which remain friendly to it by standing firmly against the pan-Arab, pro-Soviet, anti-Israel trend in the Arab world, and by attempting to reverse it. In this case success would depend largely on the vigour and speed with which the policy was pursued and the self-confidence and nerves of those advancing it. Alternatively, the United States can play for safety and try to stanch the drain of political leverage in the region and the consequent endangering of its investments and prestige by tacking as near to the wind of neutrality and political indefinition as possible in the matter of the Arab–Jewish conflict and, at the same time, carefully weaning the Russians away from their involvement in it.

The uncertainties and dangers implicit in either course are plain to see and the final choice is therefore bound to be partly a function of the kind of formula that can be made to emerge from interdepartmental debate in Washington and the collective temperament, style, and intellectual predispositions of the reigning policy-makers. Much also depends on the accepted view of the nature and dynamics of the Israel–Arab conflict itself. Yet in the final analysis, it may be supposed that the really decisive factor is the importance the United States attaches to global (as distinct from regional) considerations in general, and to the containment of the Soviet Union in particular.

In fact, it is abundantly clear that the United States, under President Nixon, is firmly set on the second course of action and the briefest consideration of the contemporary climate of opinion in Washington (and in the United States as a whole) shows why this must be so.

It is not difficult to see why the second course of action is likely to be the most congenial to a large and complex bureaucracy. The natural tendencies of any bureaucracy—to play for safety to attempt to moderate internal contradictions of policy; to avoid powerful, goal-oriented drives which would alter the environment in which it is proposed to operate, and which may fail (as in Vietnam), carrying all concerned to their political graves; to iron out departmental differences by striving for consensus—all these are inevitable unless the bureaucracy is galvanized and re-directed by an immensely powerful and determined political leader (like President Johnson before his fall) against the background of some over-riding national crisis. However, President Nixon's administrative style is one which confirms and strengthens the bureaucratic approach. It is orderly, systematic, and impersonal. Characteristically, he has revived the National Security Council machinery which both Kennedy and Johnson ignored or neglected. And it is revealing that on assuming power his first step was to call for a systematic review of major problems of foreign policy (with Vietnam and the Middle East, in that order, at the top of the list), upon which all agencies embarked on the production of analyses and on their co-ordination one with another. Under President Nixon, policy decisions are arrived at on the basis of a formal and orderly procedure. Meetings are carefully prepared, agendas 'are cleaned and scrubbed'. Rough edges tend to be ironed out. All in all, there is a conscious and methodical employment of the *machinery*. Compromise, even-handedness, moderation, legality, and a kind of prim self-satisfaction are the values which tend to inform the proceedings. There is little room left for taking relatively high, calculated risks, for the application of political surgery, and for that fair measure of simple bloody-mindedness which the alternative policy option would assuredly require.

Caution, delicacy of approach, intricacy of analysis, and the attempt to obtain optimum results in a given predicament, rather than to alter the terms of the problem itself, all tend, in their turn, to reinforce the particular view of the Arab–Israel conflict which is generally accepted and acceptable in Washington. It is not a modern view, relatively speaking, and is to be found at its finest and most lucid in that classic of the genre, the Report of the Royal [Peel] Commission on Palestine of 1937.

Manifestly the problem cannot be solved by giving the Arabs or the Jews all they want. The answer to the question 'Which of them in the end will govern Palestine?' must surely be 'Neither'. . . . From the earliest days of the British connexion with India and beyond, the peace of the Middle East has been a cardinal principle of our foreign policy; and for the maintenance of that peace British statesmanship can show an almost un-broken record of friendship with the Arabs. It is no less desirable now than it has always been that this friendship should not be impaired. On the other hand, it is clearly a British interest to retain, as far as may be, the confidence of the Jewish people wherever they are. We valued it highly in the War and we cannot disdain it in peace. . . . deadlock . . . irreconcilable . . . On the one hand . . . and on the other. . . .[31]

In a word, symmetry. Look hard at both sides, separate out the 'myths' and the 'realities' entangled in the positions of each, en-courage the 'moderates' in contradistinction to the 'extremists' in either party, and hope that with a combination of clear-mindedness, courage, reasonableness, and, above all, an ability to distinguish true interests from false on all sides, a compromise solution can be attained. In the meantime, the proper function of the extra-regional power is to keep its head above the mêlée and avoid partisanship. In the short term, such neutrality will reduce the damage to a minimum. In the middle term, it will facilitate a settlement. In the long term, it will enable the extra-regional power to reap on all sides the benefits of its caution and good intentions.[32]

The inherent virtue of such a view of the Arab–Israel conflict is that it implicitly recognizes its essentially autonomous character and discounts the fashionable but superficial view of it as a stage on which a primary power, nuclear-age confrontation is being played out through well controlled local intermediaries. Its error lies in mistaking the mechanical symmetry that is entailed by the very fact of conflict for a symmetry of internal structure and purposes. It is not difficult to show that the structure and purposes of each side, in so far as they are amenable to generalization, differ profoundly. Yet the impulsion to minimize the differences and fit the parties into a framework that indirectly implies the viability of a neutral, solution-seeking posture is apparently irresistible. Ambassador Yost, a distinguished American diplomat and one well acquainted with the Middle East (if only on the Arab side), even finds exactly the same number of 'principal myths' on each side: six.[33]

Finally, for the cautious, neutralist policy to be fully tenable, certain assumptions about the Soviet Union both as a global factor and as a Middle East power must be made and justified. It is neces-

[31] Palestine Royal Commission, *Report*, Cmd. 5479, H.M.S.O., London, 1937, pp. 374–5.
[32] For a modern epitome of this approach see Charles Yost, 'Israel and the Arabs', *The Atlantic*, January 1969, reprinted in *Survival*, June 1969.
[33] Ibid.

sary to assume that the Soviet Union is prepared to take a view of the Arab–Israel conflict that is not too far from that taken by the Americans: namely, that the Russians recognize that the dangers of paddling in Middle East waters outweigh the advantages. It is also necessary to assume that the Soviet Union, in enlightened pursuit of its own interests, will see the benefits of making common cause with the United States, de-fusing the conflict—at any rate so far as its international ramifications go—and cordoning it off, so to speak, as a preliminary to working for its final settlement. In brief, present American policy rests on the implicit assumption that, in the terms of the present argument, the Soviet Union will be prepared in certain circumstances to break off—or at least greatly attenuate—its working alliance with militant pan-Arabism.

There can be very little question that the Soviet Union's alliance with the leading pan-Arabist states presents the Russians with difficulties and contradictions, along with the advantages of added leverage. Nor can there be any question that Russia has a standing interest in entering into forms of dual international authority with the United States. Nor again, that contemporary American administrations are now in principle prepared to concede parity and that the more critical and potentially damaging the problem, the more readily concessions will flow. But the nub of the present argument is that Soviet difficulties are in great measure a result of the American ability to constrict their freedom of manoeuvre in the area. Accordingly, while it is certainly conceivable that the Soviet Union might be got to enter into a jointly-sponsored regional arrangement with the United States as a consequence of a vigorous and successful American effort to confine it, it is questionable whether it could be persuaded to enter into an understanding to spare the United States the costs of such an effort—which is what the policy of neutrality and playing for safety amounts to. Is it not more probable that, on the contrary, the very delicacy of the balance on which such a policy is necessarily founded will serve to invite the Russians to upset it—and so, in the final analysis, encourage them to persevere in the underlying effort to exclude the United States from the region altogether? Thus it is at least arguable that in the Middle East the active pursuit of an understanding between the primary states is likely to carry within it the seeds of its own failure.

Alternatively, the United States must rely—deliberately or unconsciously—on Israel itself. As has been argued, the dynamic of the Arab–Israel tier of the conflict impels Israel to apply all available strength to the frustration of the Arabs first of all, but also indirectly, to the frustration of the Soviet Union. It follows that the more the United States tends to relax direct anti-Soviet pressures, the more it will tend to rely on Israel to maintain them on its account. The prospect of a palpable disengagement from Israel would then come to rely, paradoxically, on the success of those Israel policies from which the United States is ultimately intent on disassociating itself.

(4) There are three salient points to be made in discussing the role the two primary powers play in the Israel–Arab conflict and in considering the role the lower tier of the conflict plays in the pattern of relationships between them. First, neither of the two primary powers has significant influence on the internal dynamic of the regional conflict—if only because the disputants, Arabs and Jews, attach greater value to the achievement of the respective goals and to the frustration of their opponents than to their relations with that primary power on which they have tended to rely. True, Arabs and Jews have qualitatively different goals. While the Arabs have come to see the liquidation of Israel as a moral and political imperative, the Jews see Israel's maintenance and reinforcement as a matter of national life and death. Achievement of the first goal can be acceptably postponed; not so the second. Accordingly, the ability of the Soviet Union (or any other considerable extra-regional force) to deflect the Arabs from their course in the short term, may be greater than the ability of either power to deflect Israel. But on neither side is the relationship adequately summed up by the term 'client' or 'protégé', as contemporary fashion would often have it.

The second point is that the policies and interests which the great powers pursue within the framework of the regional conflict are essentially incompatible with those dictated by fundamental considerations of global nuclear strategy. Involvement in the Middle East conflict incurs risks of confrontation which on other grounds the primary powers would certainly wish to avoid. And further, by exacerbating rather than lubricating the relationship between the super-powers, involvement in the conflict makes agreement on matters which cut much nearer the bone even more difficult to conclude. On the other hand, when considerations arising out of their direct, bilateral relations are to the fore and they are impelled to co-operate, if only to negotiate a policy to be pursued in the short term (as when the Six Days War broke out), what the co-operation and the understanding actually entail in terms of immediate Middle East politics is a disconnection or disengagement from their respective partners. And for this a price must be paid in due course. Furthermore, if the immediate aftermath of the Six Days War can serve as a guide, the price is apt to be a short-term intensification of partisan involvement in an attempt to offset the loss of confidence. Nevertheless, the fact that the primary powers pursue a wide range of goals, some of which bring them into conflict with each other, while others impel them towards concessions and agreement, is a cardinal element of Middle East politics as it is of politics elsewhere. It sets certain broad limits to involvement; and it suggests an obvious point of equilibrium towards which the primary powers tend (without necessarily reaching it), so long as neither has renounced the game totally. It may also be said, parenthetically, that if the conflict between Arabs and Jews were of a roughly similar nature, i.e. pursued on the basis of a range of *mixed* motives on either side, it too would tend towards some point of equilibrium and the two points of equilibrium—regional and extra-regional—might ultimately be made to coincide. But the Arab–Israel conflict is so structured that nothing remotely equivalent to the kind of middle ground which the primary powers might find to rest upon—a division into demarcated spheres of influence, agreed withdrawal from the scene, a general arms embargo, and so forth—is really conceivable. To put it bluntly, despite their heavy involvement in the region the primary powers remain relatively free to exclude the Middle East from the area of systematic conflict between themselves, should they find it expedient, and it is not impossible to envisage situations in which they might wish to cut their losses and withdraw. But the Middle East states are not free to turn the battle off and on at will or to re-direct their attention elsewhere for any length of time. And it is, perhaps, for this reason that, as compared with the immediate parties to the conflict, the behaviour of the great powers has a perennially un-certain, even indecisive, aspect.

All this seems to suggest a third, essentially speculative point. So far as the primary powers are concerned, three broad outcomes can be posited. The United States, geographically the more remote and sociologically the less disposed to continue the struggle, may gradu-ally give up; or the primary powers may both tire and agree to cordon off the region with a view to retrenchment and consolidation of existing assets; or else the intricate, indirect, and costly struggle round the central focus of the Arab–Israel conflict will continue in modes not unlike those in which it has been pursued in the Middle East since 1954/5. What all three outcomes have in common—in effect, what characterizes the involvement of the primary powers in the conflict—is that none is likely to affect the sources of the conflict itself. It may be damped down for a while, as it was between 1956 and 1964. But in all essentials the conflict will remain in being regardless of the primary powers and so will both sides' perpetual quest for military supplies which they cannot produce for themselves, for economic aid, and for international political support—in a word, for allies and confederates.

Broadly speaking, the constants of the entire system are the policies and purposes of the local disputants, while the major variables are the policies and purposes of the extra-regional powers. It is not surprising that there have been periodic variations in the relations within the two sets of regional and extra-regional powers and that these have engendered successive waves of dissatisfaction and distrust. Certainly, there is no cause to believe that the current pairing off is entirely stable, let alone immutable. In both instances it is fundamentally opportunistic. Such factors as ideological and cultural affinity, or the lack of it, are certainly of the greatest possible importance as *reinforcements* to a political association between the United States and Israel and between the Soviet Union and the leading pan-Arab states. But they are unlikely to operate very powerfully as countervailing forces if the Israelis and Arabs find that they no longer benefit from the association. Arabs and Jews remember only too well that each of the primary powers, not excluding the now defunct members of the class, Britain and France, has chosen to change sides over the past twenty to thirty years, in some cases more than once, some relatively mildly and marginally, some dramatically and blatantly.

It seems, therefore, that the Middle East primary power/minor power system is inherently less stable than it might now appear; and, moreover, that regardless of whether the primary powers come to a horizontal understanding between themselves or not, the gradual decomposition and concomitant re-ordering of their existing vertical ties with the minor powers may already be in progress. It is unlikely to go as far as a straightforward reversal of alliances. The Soviet Union has advanced too far. The United States may be too weary to do more than irresolutely dig in its heels from time to time in the sands of the Middle East. The great political conundrum for all states of the region is likely to remain a question of how they can ultimately stabilize their relations with the Russians. And this is a problem which those who fear and oppose their penetration of the area must now face, no less than those who have welcomed and facilitated it.

(5) On what terms the Middle East states—the Arab as well as the Jewish—are ultimately to stabilize their relations with the Soviet Union is part of the general problem of how the conflict between them is to evolve. But it is equally and simultaneously the greatest of the discrete problems that confront each of the states of the region over and beyond the immediate conflict. The Arabs face the question of whether and to what extent they will be able to extricate themselves from their alliance with the Russians when and if they choose

to do so. As a matter of practical politics, however, this question is still below the horizon. Without Russian assistance their hope of extirpating Israel loses whatever validity it might otherwise have. For Israel, on the other hand, the question of relations with the Soviet Union looms ever larger and is already well above the horizon. Essentially, it is the question of how far the pursuit of ends *vis-à-vis* the Arabs can be sustained in the face of steadily mounting Soviet opposition on the one hand and uneven and uncertain American support on the other. As for the Russians, the evolution of the Middle East conflict has caused Israel to become a growing obstacle to the smooth achievement of Soviet goals in the Middle East and, even more acutely, a hindrance to efforts to consolidate what has already been achieved, whether in accord with the United States or not. The defeat of the Arabs in the 1967 war changed Israel, in Soviet eyes, from an entity towards which it was politic to pursue and display hostility into one towards which it became necessary to do so.

Were the United States, following France, radically to revise its view of where the balance of its interests lay and seek a well-nigh unconditional accommodation with the Russians and the Arabs—then the character of the Russo–Israel duel would duly change. From a complex, partly indirect conflict continually refracted through the mitigating presence of the United States it would turn into a relatively straightforward confrontation much like that between Germany and Czechoslovakia after the French disavowed their undertakings.

This prospect remains somewhat remote. The United States is still trying to hold its positions; it has not fully embarked on a withdrawal —at any rate not consciously. And yet the qualitative differences between the American and Russian postures in the Middle East suggest that eventually a withdrawal will occur, if it is not already in its initial stages. It is the Russians who are after change, and therefore hold the initiative. And it is the Russians, again, who appear to attach the highest value to their Middle East positions, actual and potential, and who are prepared to make the greatest investment of human, material, and financial resources and take the greatest military and political risks. The logic of primary power politics in the nuclear age requires constant reference by all concerned to the *value* of a particular position or stance and it means that resistance to encroachment, or attempts to encroach, are effective only where the issue is highly rated by one party and understood to be so rated by the other. It follows, that the more the Russians invest in the Middle East the more seriously the Americans have to take them. And the more seriously the Americans take them, the less they will be disposed to try to reverse the process (or 'roll them back') and the more readily they will agree to make marginal concessions and retreats. In other words, the Middle East remains in great measure a 'grey' area of primary power rivalry because it is not yet evident that either super-power attaches sufficient importance to its positions there for such rivalry to be too risky to indulge in. But the successful penetration of the area by the Soviet Union is steadily reducing that proportion of the Middle East which remains effectively 'grey' and is constantly reducing the 'greyishness' of what remains. Should this process continue, as appears likely, much of the area will therefore fall in time under the undivided hegemony of the Russians and then, however unpleasant the prospect, the problem for both Jews *and* Arabs will be how to come to terms with the Soviet Union without the hidden but substantial benefit of a parallel counter-vailing American presence.

Thus whether one takes what appears to be the long-term pattern of political evolution into account, or the immediate problem set by the present active, if admittedly limited, Soviet participation in the Arab–Israel conflict, the major force Israel faces (as do the other states of the region) is now the USSR. Accordingly, and assuming Russia's successful penetration of the region to be irreversible—in the foreseeable future at any rate—Israel must now prepare to contend not only with its unique conflict with the Arabs, but with the more general problem of how an unaligned and unsupported minor state can evolve an acceptable *modus vivendi* with a great and hostile power in whose neighbourhood it happens to live.

The great exemplar of this latter problem is, of course, Finland.

CHAPTER FOUR

Finland—a Paradigm for the Future

(1) It has long been evident to the Finns that the problem of their national security is the problem of Russia and that what they have most to fear is their neighbour's massive military superiority—what Churchill called 'the dull brutish force of overwhelming numbers'. The Russians, for their part, have traditionally feared Finland's becoming, in the now standard Soviet phrase, a *place d'armes* for an attack on Russia. At the operative level of action and practical policy the conflict between the two countries has therefore tended to revolve around essentially material issues: the character of the political relationship between, previously, the Grand Duchy of Finland and Imperial Russia, and now independent Finland and the Soviet Union; and the lie of the frontier dividing them. The Tsarist state in its final stages was not merely intent on preserving Russian overlordship but was in process of demolishing the system of home rule under which Finland had been governed since its cession to Russia by the Swedes in 1809. Typically, the Russian Whites, during the Civil War, refused to recognize Finnish independence despite evident affinities with the Finnish Whites fighting their own, roughly parallel, civil war with their own Reds. The Provisional Government was only marginally less unfavourable to Finnish independence, although it did accept home rule. It was the Bolsheviks who were the most generous, at first. They recognized in Finland a strong tradition of independent and separatist political thinking, not unlike that of Poland and as likely a source of trouble if not allowed a large measure of fulfilment. 'It is unthinkable,' said Stalin, 'that we should acquiesce in the forcible keeping of any nation within the framework of any state.'[1] And it was he, as Commissar of Nationalities in the new government, who appeared in Helsinki at the end of 1917 to greet the establishment of the new state. None the less, the Bolsheviks had an eye on the strength and prospects of their sister party in Finland, engaged in its own parallel struggle for local power, and may have felt that they could

[1] Isaac Deutscher, *Stalin*, Oxford University Press, London and New York, 1949, p. 143.

afford to be generous. And despite the disappointing outcome of the
Finnish civil war, hopes for an eventual communist revolution there
were kept alive in Moscow for a very long time. It is therefore not
wholly unnatural that just prior to the outbreak of the Winter War
in 1939 the Russians should have indirectly, but none the less
plainly, resurrected the threat to reincorporate Finland bodily and
unambiguously into the Russian system by setting up the puppet
'Terijoki' government under the veteran Finnish Comintern leader,
Otto Kuusinen, taken out of the cold, in which he had languished
since 1936, for that purpose. On 1 December 1939, Kuusinen, as
Chairman of the People's Government and Minister for Foreign
Affairs announced the formation of the new Finnish Democratic
Republic. On 2 December it was accorded recognition by the Soviet
Union and the same day, in one smooth operation, a detailed Treaty
of Mutual Assistance and Friendship between the two states was
signed and published. The Russians went so far as to scour the
Red Army for ethnic Finns for a new Red Finnish Army to give
some substance to the claims made on Kuusinen's behalf and to put
a preliminary instrument of power in his hands.[2]

To this generalized, perennially overhanging threat of reincor-
poration into the Russian sphere under formal or informal suzer-
ainty there must be added the dissatisfaction both sides felt over the
location of the territorial border between the two states. When
Finland was ceded to Russia by the Swedes in 1809 the frontier
established by Peter the Great (1721) was revised as a gesture of
goodwill and Finland's 'historic' line of demarcation largely restored.
It then ran a mere 32 kilometres from St. Petersburg, but this was
of no great military consequence so long as all of Finland was an
integral part of the Russian imperial system. However, with the
independence of Finland the disquiet the Russians had always felt,
and with good reason, in the eighteenth century promptly revived
and the defensive posture on which the Bolsheviks were thrown
back under the pressure of the civil war and the foreign intervention
naturally intensified it. It reached its height with the re-emergence
of Germany as an expansionist power in the 1930s.

On 14 April 1938, a month after the *Anschluss*, the Russians
initiated secret negotiations with the Finns leading, in their final
stages, to a demand for political and territorial change. They asked
for military co-operation in the event of war in a form hardly
distinguishable from the establishment of a protectorate over
Finland and, as the talks proceeded and German political successes
multiplied, they asked for a redrawing of the frontier and for

---

[2] It folded rapidly: too few reliable and docile recruits could be found for its
political purposes to be served, let alone the military.

military and naval facilities on the Finnish shore of the Gulf of
Finland. However, the Finns refused to make more than marginal
concessions.[3] They argued then, as they were to argue subsequently,
that a hostile force could strike at Leningrad through Estonia quite
as easily as through Finnish Karelia, and that the former route was,
if anything, more probable and inviting than the latter. They feared
that once granted, Soviet bases would be used to subvert the state
from within. They saw the Russian demands as implying an
impermissible and irreversible diminution of their own still fresh
and fragile national sovereignty. They were conscious—perhaps
excessively so—of the parallel, much reiterated and popular *Finnish*
claims to those parts of Soviet Eastern Karelia which were inhabited
by kindred people. And they ascribed great importance to the
undoubted fact that they were on strong grounds legally and
diplomatically in rejecting the Russian demands. But they grossly
and fatally underrated the intensity of the Russian craving for hard
and visible barriers to attack.[4] Mannerheim, then Chairman of the
Defence Council, and Paasikivi, leader of the negotiating team in
Moscow in the final stages of the negotiations, did not so underrate
the force of the Russian motivation, but theirs was a minority view.

The stubbornness of the Finns seems to have surprised the
Russians and even shocked them mildly. In Stalin's cold eyes their
stand made no sense at all. Finland in the inter-war years had

---

[3] The most detailed and authoritative account of the matter is Max Jakobson,
The Diplomacy of the Winter War, Cambridge, Mass., 1961. See also *The
Development of Finnish–Soviet Relations*, Ministry for Foreign Affairs, Helsinki,
1940.

[4] The Soviet demands (officially in the form of 'proposals') were specific and
detailed—down to the precise number of anti-aircraft batteries (two) they
wished to emplace in the port of Hangö, itself to be leased for thirty years. What
is still more revealing—and in strong contrast to the manner in which German
political demands were being formulated at the time—is the explicit rationale.
The Soviet government stated that 'for the purpose of preserving against
external aggression the integrity of the Soviet Union coast of the Gulf of Finland
and also of the coast of Estonia, whose independence the Soviet Union had
undertaken to defend' it was necessary
(1) To make it possible to block the opening of the Gulf of Finland by means of
artillery fire from both coasts of the Gulf of Finland, in order to prevent warships
and transport ships of the enemy from penetrating the waters of the Gulf of
Finland;
(2) To make it possible to prevent the access of the enemy to those islands in the
Gulf of Finland which are situated west and north-west of the entrance to
Leningrad;
(3) To have the Finnish frontier on the Isthmus of Karelia, which frontier is now
at a distance of 32 kilometres from Leningrad—i.e. within the range of shots from
a long-distance gun—moved somewhat farther northwards and north-westwards.
(Jane Degras, ed., *Soviet Documents on Foreign Policy*, *iii*, *1933–41*, London,
1953, pp. 382–3.)

internal political and social features that were analogous to those of Czechoslovakia, but in terms of material capabilities and in international political and geopolitical position it was very differently placed. Its population was smaller, its economy was predominantly agricultural, its heartland was difficult to defend. Above all, the Finns had made nothing like the investment in military security that the Czechs had made, even in proportionate terms. On the contrary, Mannerheim's repeated demands for greater budgetary allocations for national defence had been consistently rejected and the condition of the Finnish army at the time of crisis was pitiful. 'The armed forces must at present be described as totally unfitted for war,' his Defence Council reported to the government in October 1938. A year later, in the summer of 1939, they were still without a single anti-tank gun, only 'a couple of dozen tanks, of which part were antiquated and the remainder . . . still unarmed' and with frontier defences in Karelia amounting to hardly more than a thin, sparse string of machine gun nests, unsatisfactory tank traps, inadequate pill-boxes and trenches hastily dug by students and schoolboys. (The 'Mannerheim Line' was largely an invention of Soviet propaganda designed to excuse the initial Russian reverses.) Three days before the outbreak of the war at the end of November, Mannerheim informed the President in writing that

In recent years I have found it difficult to understand the attitude of the government as well as of Parliament towards the danger which a European general war would mean to the independence of our country. While everything has pointed to a gigantic conflict approaching, the indispensable demands of our defence have been treated with little understanding and with a parsimony which left a great deal neglected. Even now, questions regarding the most urgent necessities of the armed forces are treated in as leisurely a manner as if we lived in normal times.

If the government even at this grim moment considers itself obliged to treat military matters with the same bureaucratic inertia as before, we will lose the advantages of this last respite we have been given.[5]

Again, while Czechoslovakia had at least nominal allies the Finns were unaligned in name as well as in fact, and whereas the European political and strategic position of Czechoslovakia was manifestly central, that of Finland was peripheral. Their fate could not conceivably be held a matter of vital importance—as opposed to one of moral and generalized (and diffuse) political concern—to any of the other major powers. Nor could friendly powers have given them decisive assistance even had they chosen to do so. When the question of an Anglo-French expeditionary force was discussed at the beginning of 1940 the Finns rightly (if somewhat belatedly) judged

, [5] C. G. Mannerheim, *Memoirs*, New York, 1954, pp. 296, 305, 319.

the plan insufficient, tardy, and conceived more as a means of securing Allied interest and pre-empting a German take-over in Scandinavia proper, than as a serious effort to offset Russian military preponderance. Indeed, the frivolity of the treatment of the Russo-Finnish conflict by the remaining European democracies, neutrals and belligerents alike, is typified by the condition imposed by the Swiss and accepted by the other members of the League of Nations that nothing be said at Geneva about the major war in the west while the minor one in the east was being discussed. In circumstances such as these there was really nothing to be expected from anybody. It was only in the one crucial respect that they were quite alone that the Finns' situation was identical to that of the Czechs. And somewhat like the Czechs, it took a while before they fully realized its full implications.

The tardiness of the Finns in waking up fully to the threat from Russia owed something to their success in beating their local allies off during the civil war and something to the general climate of opinion in Europe between the wars in which suspicion of the Soviet Union tended to be mixed with underestimation of Soviet capabilities. But it owed still more to the Finnish habit of looking to Germany for backing against the immediate neighbour. The tradition of sheltering behind the endemic Russo-German hostility had profound roots reaching well back into the Tsarist period and was founded, on the face of it, on a not unreasonable view of the politico-strategic situation in the Baltic region. As a basis of practical policy, however, this view of the matter had two particular and major flaws. The first was that Russian interest in Finland was above all else a function of the perceived German threat to Russia. It followed, that the more powerful Germany became, and the more active it was in the Baltic specifically, the more likely were the Russians to seek to pre-empt the Germans in the Baltic states, Finland among them. Thus the more frequent and public were Finnish sidelong glances towards Germany, to say nothing of their occasional concrete attempts to call the Germans in to redress the Russo-Finnish balance, the more strongly were Russian suspicions of Finland aroused and the more strongly were they confirmed in their belief that they must prevent the Germans from getting a toe-hold in Finnish territory by getting one there themselves beforehand. In reply to the Finns' repeated and well meant protestations that in the event of war they would maintain their neutrality and defend themselves from German encroachment no less than from any other, the stock Soviet reply was that it was beyond their power to do so. Finland was too small and too weak to stave off the Germans;

the Russians would have to do so for them. And they told them so
in so many words.[6]

The second flaw in the attempt to rely on Russo-German rivalry
lay in the changed circumstances of 1939. On 23 August the
German–Soviet non-aggression pact was signed. It was not immediately clear to the general public what was implied; and as Marshal
Mannerheim put it, 'the faith of the Finnish people in the value of
Finnish–German friendship was, in spite of all, so strong that a
wide circle regarded the non-aggression pact as being a *stabilizing
factor* in Finland's relations with the Soviet Union'.[7] At that stage,
August 1939, the general public in Finland still knew nothing about
the secret negotiations with the Russians that had been going on
since April of the year before. But to those who did, it now became
clear, if it had not been before, that like the other Baltic states into
which Russia was then moving and like Eastern Poland which it
proceeded to invade in concert with Germany, Finland had fallen
into the Russian sphere in which the Germans, by the terms of the
pact, had undertaken not to interfere. And, indeed, the Germans
kept to that part of the agreement throughout the Winter War, even
to the extent of preventing the Italians from supplying arms to
Finland. As for the Russians, while they had been granted a free
hand for the moment, their underlying fear of Germany had only
been intensified by the new partition of Poland and had acquired a
great deal more to feed on. All in all then, the Finnish concept of
balance between the two primary powers of the day lost in 1939
whatever vestigial validity it had retained till then while the root
causes leading to Russo-Finnish confrontation remained very much
alive. True, the entente with Germany came briefly to life again
after the invasion of Russia by the Germans and the concomitant
renewal of hostilities between the Russians and the Finns during
the so-called Continuation War (1941–4). But the upshot was a
longer and still more costly period of fighting (ultimately against
the Germans as well as the Russians), a more drastic territorial
settlement than that which had been imposed in 1940 (only this time
with the somewhat uncertain approval of the Western democracies),
and the seemingly final isolation of Finland within the Soviet sphere.

The ultimate defeat of Germany thus had much the same result
as the Nazi–Soviet non-aggression pact which had heralded its
brief triumph. It left the Finns alone with the Russians; and because
the crushing and dismemberment of Germany had been offset in

---

[6] As early as 1935 a Soviet envoy had officially informed the Finnish Prime
Minister that were war to break out between Russia and Germany, Russia would
occupy Finland.

[7] Mannerheim, *Memoirs*, p. 306. Italics added.

their view by the entry upon the European scene of the United States, to which the greater part of Germany was soon to be allied, the Russians were no more disposed after 1945 than they had been in 1939 quite to put aside their fears of foreign attack. Moreover, the division of Europe into spheres of preponderance remained and was soon to become more pronounced and complete than ever. So even if the Finns had been tempted to seek a neutral haven between the Americans and the Russians, they now clearly had no chance of finding one. The Americans and the British, the latter, if anything, more readily than the former, had at an early stage of the war accepted Russian preponderance in Eastern Europe and the legitimacy, as they saw it, or at any rate the inescapability, of Russian insistence on a very wide margin of territorial defence for their north-western borders—one that clearly included all the Baltic states.[8] They were prepared to argue with the Russians about a great many issues, but not about Finland. The American point of view was put plainly to the Finns, and without delay, as soon as the fighting had died down and diplomatic relations were restored.

The U.S. was allied with the Soviet Union and Great Britain, and was committed to collaboration in the war and in building a durable peace. While some Americans thought some years ago that cooperation with [the] Soviet Union was not possible, the American people and Government now stood wholeheartedly for enduring cooperation with the Soviet Union. As a neighbour to the Soviet Union I thought it especially important that Finland develop good neighbourly relations with the Soviet Union.[9]

Thus the newly arrived American Diplomatic Representative in Helsinki to the Finnish Foreign Minister in March 1945.

(2) It is against this background that the cornerstone of Finnish policy since the end of the war has been established as the acceptance of the unqualified need to 'develop good neighbourly relations with the Soviet Union'. But they have preserved themselves from the indignity and futility of mere obeisance to the Russians by setting out, from the start, to establish a relationship founded on Russian needs no less than on their own and seeking compatibility between

[8] See, for example, Eden's comments on the matter as early as January 1942 (Earl of Avon, *The Eden Memoirs*, ii, London, 1965, pp. 318–199) for an indication of how early the British had made their minds up on the subject. They were consistent in their approach right through to the negotiation of the peace treaty with Finland in Paris in 1946. For an account of the mild and, on the whole, futile attempts by the Finns to get the Western powers to help modify the harsh terms demanded by the Russians see Max Jakobson, *Finnish Neutrality*, London, 1968, pp. 22–32.

[9] *Foreign Relations of the United States, 1945*, iv, Washington, 1968, p. 605.

H

the two. The first article of the new faith was—and remains—that Russia's interest in Finland has always been predominantly strategic and that therefore the greatest and most dangerous cause of conflict between the two countries could be removed once the Soviet Union considered 'its primary strategic interests in the direction of Finland to be safeguarded'. This principle has rested on the belief that Russian fears of Germany are real and have to be respected and their consequences faced: 'I have read in the history of Russia/the Soviet Union that it has been attacked fourteen times in the last 150 years and that the capital of White Russia, Minsk, has 101 times been in enemy hands'.[10] Indeed, in a limited way, the principle could be seen at work even at the height of the war when Mannerheim, in the face of considerable public pressure at home and very heavy and repeated pressure from the Germans, refused again and again to move against Leningrad lest he thereby confirm once and for all the validity of Russian fears. 'It was my firm opinion that such an undertaking was against the interest of the country, and from the beginning I had informed the President of the Republic and the government that under no circumstances would I lead an offensive against the great city on the Neva.'[11]

But whereas Mannerheim's had been a minority and somewhat unpopular view during the war, much as it had been before the war, the postwar 'Paasikivi-Kekkonen Line' rapidly acquired the status of orthodox doctrine.

The second article of their faith is the conviction that it is necessary for the Finns to reassure the Russians regularly of their goodwill and fixed refusal to give aid and comfort to Russia's actual or potential enemies. To this has been added the corollary that if they can gain Russian confidence they can avoid close and controlled confinement within the Russian system on the Polish or Czechoslovak model (to say nothing of the Lithuanian, Latvian, and Estonian), and retain an acceptable form of what might be termed supervised and conditional liberty. Broadly, this has been achieved. But the costs of the arrangement and its impact on the general pattern of Finnish affairs in both the domestic and the external contexts has been severe.

The most obvious result at home has been the now well-established link-up of the party-political composition of successive governments in Helsinki to the Russo-Finnish *modus vivendi*. Occupation of key government positions by politicians who faithfully follow the 'Paasikivi-Kekkonen Line' is understood by both Russians and Finns to constitute the best possible evidence of

[10] President Kekkonen, speech at Vaasa, 6 January 1967.
[11] Mannerheim, *Memoirs*, p. 416.

Finland's intentions to abide by the post-1945 rules. Contrariwise, where a domestic political change is in prospect the Russians may be expected to wish to change the rules—i.e. replace parole, as it were, by confinement. Confinement being not only unattractive in itself, but liable to be irreversible, the Finns have preferred, partly by tacit agreement and consensus and partly by the tough-minded manipulation of their own system by their own leaders, to adjust the domestic scene in sufficient measure to allay Russian suspicions—and, incidentally, give the Russians first-rate evidence of *their* own ability to manipulate Finland within narrow, but adequate limits.

The two classic instances of such an adjustment occurred in 1958 and in 1961. In the first case, a new government had been formed, led by the Social Democrats. The Russians mistrusted the Social Democrats, however, and made their disapproval plain: their ambassador was withdrawn and trade agreements were suspended. President Kekkonen, after some hesitation, thereupon caused the new coalition to break up by insisting on his own supporters leaving it, and then reappointed them as a minority government. There was no doubt in anyone's mind about the major purpose of the exercise, and it was generally accepted as unavoidable. It nevertheless caused great bitterness which the internal political benefits accruing to Kekkonen's followers tended to keep alive.

In the second case, in 1961, with both parliamentary and presidential elections in the offing, the Social Democrats—whose private war with Kekkonen had naturally been intensified by the first affair—had resolved to promote their own candidate for the presidency, Olavi Honka, in alliance with other opposition parties. From the Soviet standpoint the possible emergence of the Social Democrats at the presidential level was an even more serious matter than their actual emergence at the governmental level had been three years before. The role of the president in the making of Finnish foreign policy is a central one. In law, 'the President shall determine the relations of Finland with foreign powers'.[12] In practice, unless a President is prepared deliberately to delegate his authority (as President Kallio had tended to do), Finnish foreign policy cannot fail to be strongly marked by the personality and predilections of the Head of State; and all concerned, not least the leaders of the Soviet Union, have grown accustomed to the tradition. The prospect

[12] Article 33, Constitution Act of 1919. The President requires the approval of Parliament for major acts of formal policy: declaration of war, conclusion of peace treaties. And he must operate, in practice, through the Foreign Minister. Nevertheless, there has never been any question that his voice is expected to be the predominant one, much as it is expected to be in Fifth Republic France.

of a change in the presidency in the coming (1962) election coincided, moreover, with substantial tension in east–west relations over Germany and strident, but not wholly artificial, Russian claims that the German threat was once again real. In the event, the overt Soviet response to the possibility of change in Helsinki was to call for Soviet–Finnish military staff talks under the terms of the 1948 Treaty of Friendship, Co-operation, and Mutual Assistance. They had 'full confidence in Finland's foreign policy', the Soviet Foreign Minister, Gromyko, told his Finnish colleague, Karjaleinen, but they

could not fail . . . to take note of the fact that the political situation in Finland had become unstable. A political grouping had formed with the ntent of preventing the continuation of the present foreign policy. The Soviet Government, therefore, wished to assure itself without delay that the present foreign policy would in fact prevail and that nothing would happen to disrupt the friendly relations between Finland and the Soviet Union.[13]

President Kekkonen was on a visit to the United States when the crisis broke. He was aware that he had gone a very long way towards leading his country out of the shadow which its special relationship with Russia had cast on relations with the Western democracies and he was anxious to avoid the staff talks and the implied participation in, and validation of, the Soviet Union's anti-German and anti-American front. But nor did he wish to quarrel with the Russians. Once again, he attempted to adjust the matter by internal manipulation. He called parliamentary elections five months early, confident that the opposition would be thrown into disarray, as indeed it was, and that the election results would allay Russian suspicions. When the Russians still hesitated he flew to Novosibirsk for a suitably dramatic—and now celebrated—meeting with Khrushchev. He was then successful. The request for military staff talks was withdrawn and Khrushchev proclaimed himself satisfied with a Finnish undertaking to keep watch in the Baltic area and report untoward developments. Meanwhile at home the prospective presidential candidate to whom Moscow had objected withdrew his candidature, Kekkonen's enemies arguing once again that he had exploited his status as *persona gratissima* in Moscow in his own, and his party's, political interest. In fact, the tie between foreign and domestic affairs was again proved an indissoluble one—with the former, as the orthodox view had always insisted, having clear priority over the latter. The point was later put by Kekkonen himself with characteristic bluntness:

[13] Jakobson, *Finnish Neutrality*, pp. 74–5.

Foreign policy takes precedence over domestic politics in Finland and it must do so. If we are not capable of pursuing a foreign policy consistent with our national interests, the question of a good or poor domestic policy is irrelevant. It is often difficult in practice to draw a line between questions of foreign policy and domestic policy. The scope of foreign policy has doubtless also expanded. The totality of the cold war has given many questions which were earlier purely of internal interest a foreign policy connotation. Consequently, more and more issues and solutions must be reviewed also from the standpoint of foreign policy.

Another division which is sometimes made in our country is the division between the foreign policy pursued by Government leaders and the personal foreign policy views expressed by individual citizens and politicians. There should be no such division if we desire foreign countries to believe in the sincerity of our neutral policy. Our neutrality does not, naturally, extend to the ideological sphere: our neutrality does not mean that we would abandon the defence of Finnish democracy. But we cannot plead our right to remain neutral if in the next breath we assume biased attitudes to international politics. I do not want to claim that such attitudes are common in our country, but even a few cases of the kind, especially where politicians are concerned, may in a period of international tension lead to the failure of our neutral policy as a whole.

To succeed, a neutral policy requires the support of a uniform public opinion.[14]

More recently still, the embarrassing results of the March 1970 parliamentary elections (a broad shift to the right with losses not only to the communists and the left-socialists, but to Kekkonen's own party as well) led to a fresh flurry of concern both in Moscow and Helsinki, milder but not unlike, that of 1961. The immediate result was a reversal of the Finnish decision to participate in the NORDEK project for Scandinavian economic co-operation, suddenly announced only a few days before the Scandinavian Prime Ministers were due to gather to take NORDEK into its final stage. However, this time the significance of the move was broader than a simple change of political pace abroad induced by the need to compensate for a political change at home.

International co-operation and integration, notably economic integration, has in fact been the foreign field in which evident Finnish interests have most clearly run contrary to the dictates of the *modus vivendi* with Moscow and is certainly the field in which the greatest tangible sacrifices have had to be made. Finnish trade is overwhelmingly with the West: approximately two-thirds of its exports and imports go to and from Western Europe (EFTA and EEC) alone, as against a fifth to and from the Soviet bloc countries. Moreover, while forest products still account for close to two-thirds

[14] Interview with United Press International, 5 May 1963.

of all Finnish exports and over two-thirds of all the exported forest products go to Western Europe, exports to the Soviet bloc, above all to the Soviet Union, are composed predominantly of engineering products. If to these disparities is added the fact that exports as a whole account for a full fifth of the Finnish Gross Domestic Product, it can be readily seen that the economic outlet to the West is crucial both absolutely and relatively—crucial, that is to say, both for its importance as a fraction of all economic activity and for the high degree of specialization (forest products) and consequent inflexibility which characterizes it. The advantages of reducing barriers to trade with the West, and with Western Europe in particular, are therefore only too obvious.

The question that arises for Finland is to what extent economic co-operation and integration and economic ties generally can in practice be sterilized of all political significance and so be made compatible with the special relationship with the Soviet Union. At one extreme point along the range of possibilities it was, for example, evident to the Finns that they could not respond to the 1947 American offer of aid under the Marshall Plan; and at another point along the range, Finland *was* able to join the European Free Trade Area in 1961 as an Associate Member with special arrangements to facilitate its trade with Eastern Europe. But the political implications of the Marshall Plan were very great and those of EFTA extremely limited. The real difficulties arise in that sector of the range of possibilities where the political implications of economic integration are unclear or initially indeterminate.

Finland has been able to enter into a wide range of essentially technical measures of co-operation between the five Scandinavian states, such as a common passport area and labour market and an integrated social security system. The NORDEK project for economic co-operation was to take four of the states a stage further— as far as, and hopefully beyond, a customs union. Had this exhausted the implications of a Scandinavian economic union of some kind it is still probable that all would have been well. Unfortunately, for none of the Scandinavian states can a purely Scandinavian system really compensate for absence from the major European markets to the south and west; and with the failure of EFTA to establish itself as more than a temporary substitute for the EEC, the major magnet has remained the EEC itself. Now it was always clear that were any of the Scandinavian states actually to enter the EEC as full members and so link the two systems up, Finnish participation in the extension of the parallel inter-Scandinavian economic system would have had to end and the developing Scandinavian system collapse or, at the very least, be limited to its present relatively low level of achieve-

ment. And indeed, of the four, Norway and Denmark have long
been clear candidates for admission to the EEC, while Sweden, with
its sensitivity to the implications of such a step for its own neutral
posture, to say nothing of Finland's, has been reluctant fully to go
along with them. The Scandinavians as a group have thus found
themselves torn between their desire, with its deep cultural and
ideological roots, to keep together and the countervailing centrifugal
pull of evident economic benefit. The advantages that have accrued
to the Russians by letting Finland loose in the purely Scandinavian
paddock and so intensifying the respective dilemmas of each of the
Scandinavian countries are accordingly plain to see. But so are the
limits set on Finnish activity within Scandinavia and, still more,
outside it.

No secret has been made of the fact that the basis of the Finnish
decision to remain outside NORDEK is the evident risk that it
would be linked up to the EEC and that the objection to the EEC
is political, i.e. 'the present intensified aspirations to use the efforts
for the enlargement of the European Economic Community also as
a means of creating a large and unified political community of
states'.[15] Behind this again is the established Russian objection to
supposed 'NATO-supported' plans to expand it and 'turn the
European Economic Community into a "total" West Europe, that
is into an integration whose participants would be securely bound
by discipline of not only economic, but also of financial and, more
than that, political obligations under the aegis of a "supra-national
authority" '.[16]

(3) Although Sweden has had similar, if milder, doubts about the
EEC, it is important to note that Finnish neutrality differs qualitatively from that of Sweden. In tone, there is barely any evidence in
Finland of what a *Times* leader-writer has described as the self-
righteous wish to 'fulfil the instinctive urge of Scandinavia in general
and Sweden in particular to be the conscience of Europe'.[17] Finnish
neutrality is unmistakably neutrality *against* the enemies of the
Soviet Union and there is (and can be) nothing especially self-
righteous about that. The 1948 Treaty of Friendship, Co-operation,
and Mutual Assistance (extended for twenty years in 1955 along
with the handing back of the Soviet base at Porkkala, near Helsinki,
and again extended for twenty years in, and with effect from, 1970)
recognizes Finnish neutrality, but at the same time provides that
should either Finland or the Soviet Union *through the territory of*

[15] President Kekkonen, *The Times*, 7 April 1970.
[16] *Pravda*, 3 March 1970.
[17] *The Times*, 6 April 1970.

Finland be subject to aggression by Germany or any other power allied to Germany, Finland will defend itself, 'if necessary' with the assistance of the Soviet Union, and in a manner upon which both states are agreed. From the Finnish point of view, it is frequently argued, this undertaking merely underlines what the country would have to do in any case: defend itself. From the Soviet point of view, however, the emphasis is on the particular quarter from which aggression might come; and the underlying political significance of the arrangement is the implied unqualified undertaking by Finland not to associate with the enemies of Russia.

Given Russian confidence in the Finns' intention to cleave undeviatingly to neutrality so conceived in their own interest, i.e. as a solution to the problem of Finland's own security from attack and pressure from *all* quarters, the question that arises is whether Finnish political intentions can conceivably be matched by its military capabilities.

In a sense, the problem is the old one posed by Stalin in the course of the negotiations which preceded the Winter War: is not Finland too small and weak to prevent greater powers from using it and its territory for their purposes? How can it itself ensure its own neutrality? From the Russian point of view the general provision in the Treaty for Soviet assistance in case of attack is crucial, even though it is not spelt out in terms of a permanent alliance machinery, nor subject to automatic activation in stated circumstances. At the same time, the fact is—as the Russians know only too well themselves—that potential Finnish military capability is not negligible. The Finnish army fought very hard and for a time successfully against major opposition. Both in 1939/40 and in 1944 it was sufficiently effective to set the Russians before the clear alternatives of either embarking on very large-scale operations or making do with a negotiated victory which left the Finnish state and the Finnish military establishment badly injured, but essentially intact. In each case they chose the latter alternative. In Mannerheim's phrase, 'though the enemy finally broke through our lines with overwhelming strength (in 1944), the army rose again, held up the avalanche, and gave diplomacy a chance'.[18] In other words, Finland's position of independent neutrality—as opposed to that of a mere protectorate of the Russians—can make sense, but only provided that it is on the basis of a sizeable and autonomous Finnish military capability. It follows, that to the extent that the Russians take the new Finnish neutrality seriously, it is politic for them not merely to permit the Finns to equip themselves with modern weapons, but to help them to do so. And this they have done.

[18] Mannerheim, *Memoirs*, p. x.

Today, Finland is clearly unique in possessing a careful mix of Soviet, British, and French weapons, among them Soviet MiG-21 fighters and T-54 and 55 tanks, British Gnat fighters and Vigilant anti-tank missiles, and French Magister fighter-trainers and Alouette helicopters.

Given the great change in the strategic requirements of the great powers themselves since the war—notably the declining need for extra-territorial bases and the increasing reliance on submarine fleets and intercontinental ballistic missiles—the conceivable uses of Finland to a power hostile to the Soviet Union have substantially diminished. But they have not entirely vanished. Even in the relative solidity of the contemporary European system Finland possesses some incremental value to the Soviet Union, and by the same token, to the powers hostile to it. No doubt, its role in the land and sea defences of Leningrad has become largely meaningless because Leningrad can no longer be seriously threatened by forces advancing on land or sea. But the great emptiness of northern Finland makes the country a possible route for attack by land, and more particularly by air. If the area is not to be penetrated there must be evidence of its being defended. And if the Finns cannot defend their airspace, for example, the Russians will want to do so for them. If, on the other hand, they can do so for themselves, it becomes probable that they will be left alone by all concerned. It follows, therefore, that the central *raison d'être* of the Finnish military establishment is its ability to reduce the potential effective value of Finland to either of the rival primary powers to near zero by underlining the determination of successive post-war governments to prevent Finland from being drawn into the international game. The evident fact that its armed forces could, in certain circumstances, be employed against Russia itself and that the Russians are naturally aware of it, no doubt serves to make the arrangement all the more real by illustrating the substance of Finland's essential politico-military autonomy within the limits which have been indicated. In sum, the well-established view is that neutrality makes sense both for the neutral state and for the others where all can be firmly confident in the neutral's ability to constitute a firm and immovable—and therefore reliable—rock, however small, in the shifting tides of international affairs.

The significance of neutrality as a security policy solution is based on its credibility. No state can base its foreign policy on probability assumptions of future development. Slackening tension in the world naturally creates for all states, both the members of military pacts and the neutral countries, better conditions for the development of constructive co-operation. But it does not permit neutral countries to deviate from their consistent basic line against which the value of neutrality is weighed mercilessly in the incalculable fluctuations of international politics. Finland's foreign policy is firmly based on this uncompromising consistency and continuity of neutrality.[19]

(4) The post-war political relationship between Finland and the Soviet Union is now well into its third decade. From a distance it appears to have the clean, hard and yet not uncomfortable structure of a good piece of Finnish woodwork: serviceable, sensible, unsentimental. It is therefore necessary to recall that a heavy price was paid by the Finnish people before it could be put together. Sixteen per cent of the population had been mobilized in the years of fighting, seven per cent of the nation's prime manpower had been killed or permanently disabled. Under the terms of the peace settlement twelve per cent (45,864 square kilometres) of the national territory was ceded to the Soviet Union, including 285,000 hectares of farm land, or twelve per cent of all cultivated land, as were thirty per cent of the power facilities, twenty per cent of the railways, thirty per cent of the country's sawmills and cellulose factories, and so on. The evacuated numbered 420,000—thirteen per cent of the total population. Behind them was a desert.

After leaving Vyborg, we moved slowly through a devastated and deserted country. Weeds and scrub trees were growing on the abandoned farms. The houses, doorless and windowless, were obviously sinking gradually back into the new vegetation around them. When you occasionally got a glimpse into the interiors, you saw that floors were full of rubbish and offal. And you knew that the rank new vegetation still concealed thousands of live landmines.[20]

The losses—and the grim efficiency and speed with which they were made up over and above the burden of the vast reparations shipped to Russia in kind—stand as evidence of the resilience and cohesiveness of Finnish society and the power of the Finnish national idea. Since it is hard to believe that, once the decision to reject Stalin's offer of an exchange of territory in 1939 had been made, anything less than the resistance subsequently offered the Soviet Union would have sufficed to preserve Finland from the fate of the other small Baltic states, the weight of these social and moral attributes has been extraordinary. Nevertheless, for all the catastrophic proportions of the sacrifice, it was not enough in itself to make the Russo-Finnish *modus vivendi* possible. For that the Finns have to thank the Soviet Union's success in achieving a measure of control over the territories contiguous to its western borders that

[19] Prime Minister R. Paasio, speech at Turku, 20 November 1967.
[20] George F. Kennan, *Memoirs 1925–1950*, Boston, 1967, p. 282.

appears to have satisfied it. The heaviest political costs have thus
been paid by others. In a wry way, the continuation of Finnish
independence after 1944 is in part a result of the effective liquidation
of, say, the Estonians'—much, indeed, as the Swedes' success in
keeping out of the Second World War altogether was in part a
result of the failure of the Finns to do so. So the question whether
the Finnish paradigm is of wider relevance is, at one level, the
question whether Soviet behaviour and perceived interests—or
those of any other primary power, for that matter—are likely to be
broadly similar in other parts of the world to those which are obser-
vable in north-eastern Europe.

North-eastern Europe differs from other regions in at least two
major respects. In the first place, while it is an area where the
complex offensive–defensive relationship between the two great
primary states is clearly in evidence, it is one where the impact of
this relationship is, so to speak, fixed and recognized, and where,
for that reason, it has been largely excluded for the time being from
the centre of day-to-day practical politics. Neither Russia nor the
United States is in a position to gain anything there today by an
attempt to improve its cards. The slightest innovation or change
can be met with a measured response—as when the Soviet demand
for military talks with the Finns in 1961 was countered by a quiet
Norwegian threat to reconsider the decision to exclude nuclear
weapons from Norway. And the overall stability of primary power
relationships in the region is further enhanced by the fact that the
internal regimes of the Scandinavian states, including that of
Finland, are *not* on the Soviet model and that neither the external
prestige nor the internal strength of the Soviet regime is liable to
be affected by domestic developments within them—as they clearly
were likely to be by those in Hungary in 1956 and Czechoslovakia
in 1968. As has been shown, the significance of Finnish domestic
politics for the Soviet Union is essentially diplomatic and, ultimately, strategic. Moscow's benevolent interest in the fortunes of
the Finnish Communist Party is probably smaller than it is in those
of the moderately right-wing Agrarian/Centre party which has
dominated Finnish politics since the end of the war. An outright
communist success in Finland might be positively unwelcome to the
Russians. It would be incompatible with the now traditional and
well-understood forms of loose and indirect control over Finnish
affairs, for unless the new communist Finland became a thorough-
going satellite on the Bulgarian or Mongolian model the change
would be subject to reversal. And being subject to reversal it would
re-inject into Finnish domestic politics tactical considerations,
policy proposals, and personalities which have been beyond the pale

for over a generation. Moreover, the advantages, if any, of closer and more direct control over Finnish affairs through the agency of a latter-day Kuusinen would have to be balanced against the likely reverberations in the rest of Scandinavia: the possible merger of Sweden with the NATO powers and a probable qualitative change in Norway's military role in the Western alliance. They would also have to be balanced against the by no means remote possibility of a repetition of the East Berlin or Budapest risings, to say nothing of Czechoslovak-style liberalism, in Finland itself. Finally, it is evident that the United States is not yet in retreat from Europe, as it is to some extent from South-east Asia and, if more reluctantly, from the Middle East. In Europe, it has firm treaty obligations—a point of some substance in the United States, where the legalistic aspect of political questions is of enduring significance; it has none in the Middle East (leaving aside the NATO tie with Turkey). The colossal change that would come over the political and economic globe if Western Europe were to be incorporated into the Soviet system is evident to informed public opinion in America in a way that the results that might be anticipated if the Middle East were to be so incorporated are not. American economic interests, ethnic ties, political sympathies, and sheer acquaintance with the region are all infinitely greater in the case of Europe than elsewhere. Finally, the concrete advantage of being able to maintain a large military presence in an area contiguous to the Soviet Union in precisely the manner that the Soviet Union attempted, but failed to achieve in the Americas in 1962, is less central to the strategic calculations of the United States than it once was, but is still not a card to be given up lightly and without a substantial *quid pro quo*. In short, the Soviet Union in Europe is still up against a relatively firm and unyielding opponent with which it continues to have no choice but to come to terms, an opponent which has solid advantages which it can turn against the Soviet Union at will, and one which shows none of the signs of failure of nerve or infirmity of purpose which are in evidence in its affairs elsewhere. Soviet policy in Europe is still essentially and necessarily defensive. It is on this foundation that it has been possible to maintain the subtle Russo–Finnish *modus vivendi* and it is one which is clearly absent in the Middle East, to say nothing of South-east Asia.

North-eastern Europe differs from other regions of rivalry between the primary powers in a second, perhaps still more obvious, but crucial respect. The minor states of the region are either essentially at peace with each other and by and large satisfied with the *status quo* or else have been totally incorporated in the Soviet system and lost all capacity for independent action. There are clearly no intra-regional conflicts which are even remotely of the kind which dominate the scene in South and South-east Asia, or Africa, or the Middle East or, if less blatantly and dramatically, Central America. The free Scandinavian states neither require the backing and intervention of the extra-regional powers in the settlement of their affairs, nor present the extra-regional powers with the kind of opportunities—and difficulties—to which the Arab–Jewish conflict and the intra-Arab divisions give rise. The participation of the other (non-Scandinavian) countries on the Baltic littoral in intra-regional affairs is directly determined by the preponderant power (Russia) itself.

Nevertheless, at another level of analysis the Finnish paradigm remains of permanent practical as well as speculative interest. It represents a solution without any obvious contemporary parallel to the problem facing an isolated, minor state pitted against a great military power and it remains a considerable political achievement which has been maintained in working order by all concerned for over a generation. As such it calls attention to a range of possibilities in the minor power–great power relationship which are sufficiently familiar in the case of the United States in *its* area of prime influence (Latin America), but which do not generally come to mind as attainable in the case of the Soviet Union or China.

It has been argued here that the broad tendency in such an area as the Middle East, where the relative hold and influence of the great powers is uncertain and which is therefore subject to perpetual dispute between them, is to fall slowly under the preponderance of a single power—in this case the Soviet Union. An equivalent, although more intricate and probably more gradual process can be delineated in South-east Asia, probably under China. This is to say, that in crude terms, some of the dissimilarities between these areas and Eastern and Western Europe will be reduced in time as the relative fluidity and ephemerality of position and alignment which characterize them give way to solidified spheres of great power control. The political survival of a minor state as something more than an object of policy would then depend first and foremost on its ability to manipulate—or manoeuvre within—a balance of restraint and pressure between it and the preponderant power in whose sphere it falls, as does Finland, rather than on a complex balance built up out of the interplay between all the forces in the arena, as do Israel, or Egypt, or North Vietnam, or Cambodia.

CHAPTER FIVE

Options and Policies

Each of the three paradigms discussed in the preceding pages is a case of international conflict, the framework and broad character of which are determined by the fact that at least one of the parties to the conflict has both the will and the capacity to employ force. At the same time, each of the three cases concerns the confrontation of a state of limited material and human resources with one which commands resources that are very much greater. As such, the three paradigms belong to a category of international conflict in which the outcome tends to be predictable and which is further marked by the fact that the disparity of material resources greatly reduces the intellectual and moral demands made on one party (the powerful) while raising those made on the other party (the weak) to their highest.

It is true, and important, that in the case of Czechoslovakia, the immediate disparity between minor power and great power was unusually small, with the Czechoslovakia of 1938 representing, perhaps, the limit of strength to which a state that is 'small' by almost any standard[1] can have attained. Yet the fact that Czechoslovakia was able to meet Germany with roughly equal military capacity in September 1938 is, in a sense, a curiosity of history—and of timing. A year later the steadily expanding German army would certainly have been considerably stronger than Czechoslovakia, had the latter still been in existence. It is therefore arguable that had war between the two broken out at the end of September, had it not turned rapidly into a general European war, and had all other relevant factors remained constant (such as the relations between Hitler and his principal generals), sooner or later Germany would have won the contest. In fact, we have evidence today that the rumblings among the senior German generals were much more serious than was supposed at the time. And more generally, it was at least conceivable that a general European war *would* follow a major clash in central Europe involving close to three million men, and that Russia would attempt to top up Czechoslovak resources, as

[1] Cf. pp. 4-10 above.

compared with those of Germany, perhaps along the lines of Stalin's endeavour to do something of the sort in Spain. No doubt, all of this is speculative. And it is crucial that the Czechs refused to speculate. They decided to take no risks at all and to assume that all concerned—British, French, Russians, and Germans—would, in the event of war breaking out at the beginning of October and continuing throughout the winter of 1938/9, cleave undeviatingly to lines of policy adopted in the middle of September. But that decision of principle was not merely unreasonable; seen as a political decision it was absurd.

The material effect of the Chamberlain–Daladier policy of appeasing Germany was to shift Czechoslovakia from the class of states associated with Britain and France to the class of states associated with Germany, that is to say, into the politico-geographic sphere in which Germany could operate without fear of intervention from its opponents. The reversal in the French position, in particular, was thus analogous to the kind of drastic shift that would occur in the modern European system if a member of the NATO alliance were allowed to fall within the Soviet sphere. For integration of a formerly Western-orientated state within the Soviet system implies a double abandonment by the West. Not merely does it then become fair game for the hegemonic power, but it becomes a matter of concern to the rivals of the hegemonic power that the rebel state within the system should not resist pressures to bring it to heel lest the rivals themselves be swept into the ensuing maelstrom. It is in this sense that Hungarian resistance to Russia in 1956 and Czechoslovak resistance in 1968 were first and foremost sources of embarrassment and fear for the Western powers, since the more successful and determined the opposition and the greater the consequent involvement of Soviet forces and prestige, the more rapidly would the delicate structure of mutual understanding and deterrence binding the Western and Eastern systems crumble. Embarrassment was successfully staved off in both cases, of course; fear that either satellite might trigger off a global clash was decisive.

But in 1938, long before the advent of nuclear weapons, with divided public opinion in Britain and France, and with the latter facing an opponent that was both weaker militarily and more incalculable politically, resistance by Czechoslovakia was liable to have a much more forceful trigger effect on the European system than it could hope to have thirty years later. In practice almost everything depended on the Czechs themselves, on their military capabilities, and on their will to put the considerable conjunctural advantages latent in their situation to good use. Yet in the event, as has been shown, the Czechoslovak leadership approached the terrible situation which confronted them in an essentially passive spirit, politically and diplomatically. Indeed, the horrific pit into which they saw themselves falling was to some extent a product of their own excessively deferential and defensive diplomacy. Or to put the matter in the analytical terms suggested in the introductory chapter of this study, they first misjudged the *intrinsic* capabilities of Czechoslovakia as a military power as matters stood at that moment; and then compounded the error by almost total intellectual and practical political neglect of Czechoslovakia's *contingent* capabilities. In brief, all concerned, the Czechs by their excessive modesty no less than the Germans by design, the English and the French through fear, and the Russians by their reticence, combined to create that relatively rare diplomatic situation where a great, predatory power is allowed to confront its victim in a duel-like conflict despite the manifest importance of the issue to all the other powers involved.

The case of Czechoslovakia is remarkable for the extent to which successive governments and military leaders managed to build up the country's intrinsic capabilities to a scale and with such a degree of success that a duel-like conflict between that country and Germany was tenable, at any rate for a considerable period, at what seemed likely to be the moment of truth. However, so great a build-up of defensive capabilities relative to the offensive capabilities of a great opponent is unlikely to occur again; and by the same token, a simple duel-like confrontation between primary and tertiary powers is unlikely ever again to be seriously tenable. The somewhat simplistic principle that the isolated state should seek to maximize its military resources provided the net short-term effect on its economy does not reduce its capacity to maintain an adequate defence establishment in the long term, still holds in a general way. But the practical limits within which the tertiary state can operate, compared with those of the primary power, are now severely limited.

First, the contemporary distribution of nuclear weapons marks the clearest of all divides between the primary states and the others and it is a divide which is now probably unbridgeable. Such argument as there may be about the strategic merits, if any, of the possession of nuclear weapons by tertiary states is completely hypothetical,[2] not least because of the determination of the primary states to perpetuate the present limited distribution of these weapons. Their determined policy on the subject has been given formal, inter-national legal embodiment in the Non-Proliferation Treaty of 1968, which is itself the product of three years of intricate argument at the Eighteen Nation Disarmament Committee at Geneva under Russo-

---

[2] Cf. the author's *The Inequality of States*, pp. 159–82.

American leadership; and still more intricate pressures and counter-pressures behind the scenes have impelled almost all of the prominent candidates for membership of the nuclear club to adhere to it. The key provision of the Treaty—nowhere explicitly stated, but implicit throughout—is the division of the international community into two classes of states. One class, the so-called 'Nuclear-Weapon States', is envisaged as comprising those which are governed by political and military leaders who believe they require nuclear weapons and do in fact possess them. A second class, the so-called 'Non-Nuclear Weapon States', is to consist of all other states, and to be led, in effect, by governments that do not and may not control such weapons regardless of what they believe (or come to believe) to be necessary for national security. In brief, the doubts of those tertiary states which have seriously considered the pros and cons of establishing an independent nuclear capability are now matched by the manifest intention of the major nuclear powers to restrict these weapons to themselves. (China's position is, however, formally opposed to that of the United States and Russia.)

The military potential of the contemporary tertiary state is also limited relative to that of a great opponent by the ever-increasing sophistication and cost of conventional weapons. Whereas the Czechoslovak army was by no means qualitatively inferior in armament to the German army of thirty years ago, but on the contrary was generally equal to it and in some respects superior, no small state today, nor any middle power for that matter, can hope to maintain anything like qualitative parity of equipment with a primary power on the basis of its own intrinsic resources. And if it is to make a serious effort to build up and maintain forces with a view to confrontation with a great power it is to the rivals of that great power that it must turn—thereby lessening its freedom of manoeuvre and its capacity to take maximum advantage of whatever contingent capabilities and attributes it is fortunate enough to possess.

It is worth stressing once more that the political effects of modern weapons are in some respects more far-reaching than the strictly strategic effects because they tend to diminish the primary states' freedom of manoeuvre *vis-à-vis* each other in the international arena as a whole, while at the same time they increase the capacity of each to exercise authority within its respective sphere. Accordingly, conflict between the primary states, because it cannot be pursued unremittingly, tends towards equilibrium, if not actual resolution, and also towards the ever clearer demarcation of the areas which come under the political leadership and protection of each. For the rest, conflict tends to erupt and to be pursued precisely in those

I

areas which are not part of a primary power's explicitly or tacitly recognized domain, but are peripheral to it—or judged to be so. However, once conflict has erupted in a 'grey', indeterminate area, each primary power becomes acutely aware of any gain to the other side and loss to itself. It follows that a gain to one side is apt to lead to the more careful drawing of lines and the ever sharper definition of positions and interests—and hence to a loss of 'greyness'—more or less in step with the evolution of the conflict. What is then immediately at issue, as much for the minor powers of the system as for the primary powers themselves, is the rate at which the existing inconstant and reversible political associations will be replaced by public and comparatively permanent alignments and, of course, what the precise locus of the division will be. For the tertiary state, the ultimate significance of inclusion in one or other of the spheres is the decline, or even total liquidation, of its capacity to call upon one primary state for aid against another. Accordingly, where high value is attached to political autonomy, or where such a state experiences or anticipates conflict with a greater power, one long-term purpose must be the slowing down of the division and the retention of residual regional uncertainties as long as possible.

The Finno–Soviet conflict can serve as an almost perfect illustration of the present argument. It was, and continues to be, immediately relevant to our own times in ways in which the classic case of Czechoslovakia is not. The sources of Russia's impulsion to advance politically and militarily beyond the 1939 frontiers are broadly comparable to those which operate today. The disparity of forces between Finland and the Soviet Union at the time was appropriately immense. The cardinal political error of the Finns was their reliance, perhaps partly unconscious, on such traditional contingent political advantages as the German factor in the Baltic. When, in the event, the latter was neutralized by the Russo-German Pact of 1939 the vast intrinsic strength of the Soviet Union could, in theory at least, be applied to the stated Soviet purpose without inhibition.

Nevertheless, the Finns were able to extend the Winter War into the early spring of 1940, well beyond the brief campaign which the Russians had plainly envisaged as sufficient. And it was this—their capacity to put up a measure of resistance—that led to the discussion of a possible Anglo-French intervention on the Finnish side. While it was never likely to have achieved its ostensible purpose and while the prime concern of the British, in particular, was to pre-empt the Germans in Sweden and Norway, rather than save the Finns, such an intervention would certainly have complicated matters for the Russians and made it more probable that they would be drawn into the European war which Stalin was so anxious to avoid. It is therefore at least plausible that the prospect of even limited intervention was among the factors which induced Stalin to agree to end the Winter War on relatively mild terms, terms which were not a great deal harsher than the arrangements he had originally demanded of Finland.[3] Certainly, it is known that the Finns were aware of the importance of keeping the intervention project alive as long as possible, and at least until peace talks with the Russians could be started. Thus courageous resistance and a heroic if belated effort to make the most of slim intrinsic resources were combined with a delicate manipulation of equally slim and inadequate contingent resources in a successful attempt to stave off military disaster and the occupation of all Finland that doubtless would have followed it.

When we come to the case of the fully contemporary paradigm (Israel versus the Soviet Union—but equally, North Vietnam versus the United States) we see that the disparity of intrinsic resources in a genuine duel situation is enormous and that accordingly a much tighter, more complex, and more clearly understood intercalation of other politico-military factors is crucial to the ability of the minor power to sustain even limited and indirect conflict with a primary state for however short a period. The mechanism whereby political and military pressures are exerted by all concerned, thus reducing the effect of the material and political disparities and making the pursuit of conflicting policies by strong and weak states possible, is the two-tiered great power/small power conflict. But even conflict thus structured and thus mitigated is becoming difficult to sustain, because the central moderating factor—the intercalated great power rivalry—is itself inherently unstable. All things being equal, it tends either to terminate in a stalemate such that the minor regional powers find themselves irreversibly divided between the primary powers on a recognized and quasi-legitimized basis; or else it ends with the region as a whole coming under the hegemony of that primary state which has pursued the conflict with the greatest determination and has demonstrably made the greatest investment in success. Thus where the mitigating factors operate, they may appear, from the point of view of the minor power, to be ultimately self-defeating, or at best wasting assets: the minor power's room for manoeuvre becomes increasingly restricted until, in time, it finds itself for all practical purposes alone in the ring with its great opponent. The pattern of evolution of such a mitigated, partly indirect conflict thus appears to tend in the long term towards the straightforward confrontation on the Czechoslovak–German or

[3] See in this connection, G. F. Kennan, *Russia and the West under Lenin and Stalin*, London, 1961, pp. 337–8.

Finno-Russian models beyond the stage where mitigating factors intervene. Thereafter all depends on the role the small power plays in the overall purposes of the great power with which it is in conflict. Where its role is central—as was Czechoslovakia's for Germany—it will fare badly. Where its role is essentially peripheral —as is Finland's to this day—it will fare better.

It is clear, none the less, that in the interim and regardless of the precise structure of the conflict, the more single-minded and determined the minor power is in the pursuit of its ends, the greater are the costs which the primary power incurs in dealing with it. The steady rise in American participation in the Vietnam war until the decision to attempt to disengage was taken in 1969 and the equally steady, although in absolute terms, less dramatic rise in Soviet participation in the Israel–Arab war since 1967, are sufficient evidence of this functional relationship. Moreover, given that we are concerned with conflict in a region which is not (or not yet) under the hegemonic control of the primary power in question, the greater the costs it incurs the greater will be the attraction of participation from the sidelines for the rival primary power—always provided, of course, that the latter does retain an interest in containing and embarrassing its rival. All this gives the minor power a degree of influence on the structure of its conflict with the great power and also a measure of leverage which are well beyond what would be strictly proportionate to its intrinsic resources, and which enhance its political autonomy in the interim period. On the other hand, the greater the investment made by the primary power, the more rapidly does the overall significance of the conflict alter and its importance for the primary power rise.

The minor power is thus faced with mutually contradictory imperatives. Only intransigence offers it hope of retaining a measure of influence over the environment. But the more effective an opponent it becomes for the great power the heavier will be the resources the latter applies to its own political ends; and, by extension, the harder will the position of the minor power become. For once the conflict develops into a contest in the application of force, the minor power stands only to lose. What may save the situation for the minor power is the fact that the internal contradictions in the position of the great power involved in such partly direct, partly indirect, conflict are in some ways more acute. The structural expression of the intercalation of regional and extra-regional powers in a two-tiered conflict is the establishment of a coalition between one of the parties to the regional conflict and the active extra-regional power. This coalition comes to be the essential instrument of the latter's purposes; and as the conflict evolves, the coalition develops from a *de facto* alliance into an increasingly limited, one-sided protectorate. As such it is a source of mounting difficulty for the small power which is *ex hypothesi* without the benefit of equivalent protection by another primary state. For by persisting in the regional quarrel it cumulates opposition on both levels and the more successful it is at the level of purely regional conflict, the greater are the dangers it encounters at the extra-regional level. On the other hand, the great power is impelled to assume responsibility for the security of its loyal ally without acquiring an equivalent degree of political authority over it. It thus incurs a progressive fuzzing of the distinction between actions which it performs in the interests of maintaining or expanding its presence in the region and actions which it performs at the behest of its protégé because the latter cannot be allowed to founder. As a result, the primary power finds itself slowly drawn into a quasi-mercenary role; and the more uncongenial that role becomes the stronger are the grounds for liquidating the one-sided protectorate and instituting full political control. The relationship between the active extra-regional power and its local ally is thus an inherently unstable and unsatisfactory one. And as such it constitutes a target to which the minor power against which the coalition is directed has good reason to apply itself. All this can be seen in the difficult relationship between the United States and South Vietnam and the only moderately less difficult one between the Soviet Union and its Arab allies, notably Egypt.

But for all the difficulties an effort to dissolve such a coalition is unlikely to succeed if no alternative arrangement or alternative partner is in sight. The continued presence of a primary power in a 'grey' area presupposes a special relationship with some at least of the local powers. Otherwise, the 'presence' is too tenuous to be convertible into usable political, let alone military, currency. A qualitative change in the relationship, if it is not to amount to a net loss, must therefore be compensated for to be acceptable.

In principle, such compensation could take the form of a reversal of alliances. For if the partnership with one local state or group of states has turned sour and has become excessively costly, even counter-productive, partnership with the more effective and successful local rival may begin to seem attractive. At the very least, there may be advantages in making the best of a bad job and in coming to terms with the hitherto hostile local power, disengaging from the over-burdensome local ally. Thus in the abstract. In practice, a question that will arise is whether the potential partner can serve the purposes of the preponderant power. And, indeed, a small and politically isolated state, as defined here, clearly cannot. Israel cannot offer the Soviet Union what Egypt has given it and consequently the loss of influence in and over Egypt could not be adequately compensated for by the establishment of an intimate relationship with Israel. Or, to put the point somewhat differently, a *secondary* or middle range power can hope both to deter pressure from a hostile primary state to some extent and to attract support from a potentially friendly one by exploiting the change in the worldwide distribution of political, economic, and military resources that would necessarily follow its realignment. But the intrinsic resources of the *tertiary* power are too limited for it either to attract or to punish with the same facility by the simple act of realignment. By the same token, the interests, in the pursuit of which the primary power has entered into conflict with the tertiary power, are necessarily of greater weight than the latter can offset unaided. True, one conclusion that might be drawn from this is that the minor power is impelled to maximize its resources—in effect, to attempt to rise in the international hierarchy. Yet apart from the question as to whether a change of this kind is feasible, it is clear that it could only come about at the expense of other minor states within the region and in the course of a further intensification of the regional conflict, the original source of its troubles. In this sense a 'greater Israel', if established, would become a more valued and necessary potential partner to the Russians (or the Americans). But it would have the disastrous secondary result of intensifying the lower tier of the conflict (with the Arabs), probably beyond repair.

In sum, as long as the structure of the two-tiered conflict remains essentially unchanged, both the isolated minor state and the extra-regional global power with which it is in conflict are impelled to maintain courses of action which are almost diametrically opposed and to seek to thwart each other at every turn. And accordingly, so long as the conflict is thus structured, the possibility of devising a *modus vivendi* between the two is remote.

Once again the Finnish paradigm is instructive. It illustrates the uses of seeing the international possibilities of the small power in terms of its relative value to the primary state as an actual or hypothetical increment to the latter's array of total material and political resources. Since a small power is *ex hypothesi* one which cannot constitute more than a very limited, even insignificant increment, all depends on its contingent and instrumental role in the great power's scheme of things and this is, of course, first and foremost a function of the policy and behaviour of the great power itself. In northern Europe the emphasis in Soviet Russia's characteristic offensive–defensive has been fairly consistently on the *defensive* since the Revolution. Its objectives were therefore limited and—no less important—capable of relatively simple definition. Accordingly, all depended upon whether successive Finnish governments did or did not regard the safeguard of Soviet objectives as compatible with the vital interests of their own country. As we have seen, the Winter War brought about a partial change of opinion on the subject, to become decisive and, indeed, to be elevated to the level of doctrine (if not dogma) at the end of the Continuation War. In the case of Czechoslovakia versus Germany the real positions were almost the reverse of those operative for the Finns. The Czechoslovak leadership allowed itself to be persuaded that German objectives were limited and that their attainment was compatible with the minimal interests of the country. In this they were mistaken: the objectives which Germany was pursuing were manifestly aggressive and expansionist and were for all practical purposes limitless. Furthermore, the liquidation of Czechoslovakia as an autonomous political entity was itself an object of German policy—not, of course, because possession of Bohemia, Moravia, and Slovakia were regarded by the Nazi government as an end in itself, but because of Czechoslovakia's contingent political and strategic role as the key eastern ally of France and the 'aircraft carrier' blocking the German advance into eastern Europe. In the circumstances, the more profound the understanding of German policy, the less reasonably could a *modus vivendi* be envisaged.

Such is the case of a small power/great power conflict which is—or which becomes—bilateral in structure and where the small power by reason of its limited value as a potential increment has little or no influence on the broad policy pursued by the great opponent. In the case of the much more complex two-tiered conflict, however, it is rarely possible to relate the interests of great and small power directly with a view to assessing their relative compatibility.

In a two-tiered conflict, each of the states involved must operate on two distinct levels of interest and action with respect to each of the others: the regional and the global. At one level the goals pursued are seen as central to national security and the national interest. At the other level the goals are instrumental. Members of the same class of states approach each other in terms of what is dictated by the pursuit of goals that are central to national security and the national interest. Members of different classes look upon their relations with each other in terms of what is expedient in the pursuit of instrumental goals. For Israel and the Arab states the goals immediately in view in their relations with each other are central to their respective national purposes. For the United States and the Soviet Union in their relations with Israel and the Arab states the goals in view are only indirectly relevant to, are ultimately reducible to, and must be justified in terms of, global and continental considerations. It follows that for the minor, regional power an adjustment to the requirements of the extra-regional power entails what cannot but appear an incommensurate sacrifice of what is most valued in favour of what the other side regards as merely expedient—a sacrifice which is all the harder to make because, like an offering to Moloch, it may have to be repeated. This is the obvious source of the well-known and much resented inflexibility of minor powers in complex, two-tiered conflict situations and the relative tactical weakness of their great partners.

At the same time, the deeper and more protracted the involvement of the extra-regional power in the intra-regional conflict, the greater the tendency seems to be for the conflict between small and great powers to take on much of the acerbity which characterizes the regional conflict between approximately equals. In the case of the minor power this is the plain result of the growing identity of purpose between the powers arrayed against it. The deeper the involvement of the Russians in the Middle East, or that of the Americans in Vietnam, the more rapidly does the operational significance of the distinction between Russia and Egypt, to say nothing of Russian and Arab, or between South Vietnamese and American, decay—even though it does not and cannot lose all value. In the case of the great power, the growing acerbity of conflict and the slow loss of what might be termed 'instrumentality' is partly a function of the increased weight of the investment made and the importance attached to the pursuit of the stated purposes. It may be partly, too, the result of growing frustration on both sides where the powerful seemingly cannot crush the weak and the weak cannot defeat the powerful. And, finally, it is to some degree the result of the growing need of the government of the extra-regional state to justify and legitimize its operations at home and abroad in terms of what is either ideologically and morally mandatory, or vital to the intrinsic purposes and security of the state, or both. In sum, the minor power/great power conflict becomes increasingly like the intra-regional conflict on which it is founded and so ever less conducive to resolution, whether through disengagement of partnerships all round or through slow modification of policy. If nothing occurs to disturb this evolutionary pattern the outlook for the minor power becomes grim indeed.

What does all this add up to? Do any specific lines or types of policy emerge as more promising or more prudent for the small state which finds itself in conflict with a primary power, or any general criteria by which the relative merits of different policy options may be judged? What approach seems best calculated to serve the continual effort to evolve the policy which is least hazardous and most likely to protect and perpetuate the political autonomy of the small power not merely in the short term, but in the long term also?

One answer to these questions is that there is no clear and simple formula for success, even relative success, if only because in an international conflict in which force is an actual or potential factor there can be no simple and straightforward compensation for material weakness. And in the particular type of conflict with which this study has been concerned, namely that between the exceedingly strong and the comparatively weak, where the really crucial question is what *fraction* of the major disputant's total resources will be injected into the conflict, and where no possible combination of purely *autonomous* resources of men and matter and mind can decide the issue in favour of the weak, the only effective compensation can come, if at all, from outside the conflict system itself.

Nevertheless, there have emerged from the present discussion the outlines of certain general courses of action whereby the small, isolated state may sustain—or even stave off—conflict with the great state to the utmost limit permitted by its material resources. These are: (*a*) the maximization of intrinsic military potential up to, but not beyond, the divide between conventional and nuclear weapons —in order to raise the costs of conflict for the opponent to the highest possible level; (*b*) the determined, but careful use of diplomatic and, where necessary, military capabilities in an effort to make the great opponent fully and continually conscious of the high costs of conflict and of the refusal of the small state to be deflected from its objectives—provided the latter are, on other grounds, attainable; and, (*c*) the still more careful and judicious exploitation of all available contingent attributes, political as well as strategic, in an effort to lever the greatest possible auxiliary counter-pressures from outside the immediate small power/great power conflict system.

It is evident that to make policy along lines such as these is to make policy for an autonomous member of the international system and to make it, moreover, on a conceptional scale which comes close to being global: for if the policy is to succeed it must be based on reasoned consideration of the apparent interests and probable behaviour of all global powers, no less than on the assessment of the intentions of the small state's own regional rivals. To put the proposition somewhat differently, the classic distinction between great and small powers as states whose political interests and activities are respectively global and regional breaks down—or must be made to break down—when the opponent of the small 'regional' power is in fact a global one.

Nevertheless, policy conceived along these lines is policy for an interim period, though quite possibly a greatly extended one. The crucial aspect of the setting for small power/great power conflict in our times is, as we have seen, the two-tiered conflict in which two or more of the primary states are themselves involved in a 'grey' area defined as such both by the fact of great power interests in it and by the comparative indeterminacy of the status of the great powers within it. And the dynamic of great power conflict in such an area is such that while the rivalry persists, indeterminacy is lost and positions become increasingly clear and more sharply defined. For the small power itself this means drastic loss of contingent attributes and resources and concomitant loss of leverage. It may be expected that in the course of time the complex structure of its conflict with the great power will be replaced by a relatively simple, bilateral structure, with a consequent weakening of its capacity to sustain such conflicts and, ultimately, of its capacity to play a genuinely autonomous international role.

What then lies beyond the interim period? What will happen when the former 'grey' area in which the small power is placed has been divided into sub-areas where one or other of the primary powers preponderates? If speculation may be pushed so far, it would seem that several great changes in the structure of international relations within the new region are likely to occur. For the newly preponderant power the emphasis will increasingly be on the *defensive* aspects of policy, the strategic offensive, if any, being carried over to areas beyond the divide. And this development, in turn, will surely have two major consequences. One will be a change in the bilateral relations between the preponderant power and its minor opponent, the latter having been shorn, of course, of much of its capacity for autonomous action. The change will amount to a great simplification and crystallization of the matters at issue between the two states. And if, indeed, defensive considerations are henceforth uppermost in the minds of the leaders of the preponderant power, it is conceivable—as the Finnish paradigm suggests—that a not wholly intolerable *modus vivendi* between the two would be established. The second major consequence of such a transfer of emphasis to the defensive would be an altered attitude to intra-regional conflict. From being a source of opportunity it would become a source of danger, a drain on energy and strength, a continual invitation to rival global powers to sap the central position of the newly preponderant power by a process of what might be termed re-intervention. In fact, it would be reasonable to suppose that the ability to impose a political (to say nothing of military) standstill within the region would soon appear to all concerned not only as essential to the establishment and perpetuation of preponderance in the region on practical grounds, but as the central and public *test* of that preponderance. And this done—if it were done—the chances of greatly simplified and relatively irenic relations between great and small powers would be greatly enhanced.

It may further be supposed that such an evolutionary change in relations would lead, in time, to a great drop in the nervous temperature and degree of acerbity with which the conflict on all levels had been pursued and which had come to constitute the essential climate of international relations within the region and beyond. But equally, it is unlikely that such a change could take place—at any rate not before vast damage had been done to all concerned and first and foremost to the weak members of the conflict system—unless there were a prior change of attitude to the conflict itself and to relations with opponents at all levels. One of the many dangers that confront the small state locked in conflict with a far more powerful one, mitigated though the conflict may be by the inhibitory and moderating effects of the two-tiered structure, is that the passion and bitterness and fear which are at the source of the conflict at the strictly intra-regional level carry over in time to all parts of the structure. It is therefore as unrealistic to expect the embattled small power to adjust itself with any will or speed to the new state of affairs and the new, much reduced possibilities for autonomous political and military action as it is uncertain that the great power will see the value of restraint. The fact is—and it is a familiar fact—that the extraordinary intractibility of such a conflict as that between Jews and Arabs in the Middle East or that between the quasi-national/ideological/social movements which have kept Indo-China in a state of almost perpetual war for over two decades owes much to the practical unacceptability to the disputants of the rules of classic balance-of-power politics which, in their view, are also logically inapplicable. Two of the rules, as Hume showed in his celebrated essay on the subject, were that every member of the conflict system must be regarded as a potential associate, no less than opponent, and further, that no conflict may be pursued to the end.[4] If international conflict is to be mitigated, let alone resolved, it is essential that these rules are recognized once more as being both valid and desirable.

[4] The Athenians 'supported Thebes against Sparta, till the great victory gained by Epaminondas [the Theban] at Leuctra; after which they immediately went over to the conquered, from generosity, as they pretended, but in reality from their jealousy of the conquerors'. *Essays Moral, Political and Literary*, II, vii.

APPENDIX

No fully reliable figures for a comparison of the actual *autonomous* military resources of Israel and the Arab states have ever been published. The best neutral estimates are those published annually by the Institute for Strategic Studies in London. On the basis of their figures for 1969/70 (cf. *The Military Balance, 1970/71*) the following comparison of some key indicators may be made:

	Population	GNP ($ million)	Armed manpower	Combat aircraft
ARAB STATES				
Consistently involved				
Egypt (UAR)	33,300,000	6,300	288,000	415
Iraq	9,000,000	2,800	94,500	229
Jordan	2,225,000	700	60,250	38
Syria	6,025,000	1,350	86,750	210
	50,550,000	11,150	529,500	892
Occasional or partial participants				
Algeria	13,750,000	3,000	57,000	170
Lebanon	2,700,000	1,600	16,250	24
Libya	1,935,000	2,400	15,000	7
Saudi Arabia	7,300,000	3,900	36,000	75
Sudan	15,600,000	2,100	27,450	32
	41,285,000	13,000	151,700	308
Total	91,835,000	24,150	681,200	1,200
ISRAEL	2,900,000	4,500	300,000*	330

* (75,000 regular cadre and conscripts; the balance: reservists)

INDEX

Alexandrovsky, Soviet minister in Prague, 38, 47–8
Algeria, 60, 63 n., 80, 83
Anglo-French ministerial conference on Czech crisis, 21, 22, 40, 41
Anglo-French proposals for Czechoslovakia, 20, 21, 23, 25, 33, 34, 36, 41, 46, 47, 49
Appeasement policy towards Germany, 21
Arab guerrilla organizations, 72
Arab League, 62, 68
Arab Palestinian state: set up by UN 1947, 60; most annexed by Jordan, part by Israel, Gaza Strip occupied by Egypt, 60–1
Arab–Jewish wars: first, 60; second, 61; third (the Six Days War), 57, 61
Arab–Muslim tradition, 62–3
Arab States, 11, 53, 55–98, 125; their formal political independence, 59; conflict over Palestine, 59; local dissent from pan-Arabism, 59; policy to destroy Israel, 65 ff.; oil revenues, 69; unremitting hostility to Israel, 71

Balfour Declaration on Jews and Palestine (1917), 58
Beck, Colonel, 44
Beneš, Edvard, 13, 17, 18, 19 and n., 20, 21, 22 n., 24, 36, 37–8, 44, 47, 48–9, 51, 52, 53; character of, 25
Berchtesgaden, 22, 23, 43
Berlin, 18, 31; 1961 crisis, 77
Beuve-Méry, Hubert, 19 and n., 36 n.
Bohemia, 15, 29, 50, 127
Bolsheviks, 99, 100
Bonnet, Georges, 16, 20, 36 n.
Brazil, 5
Britain, 6, 7, 13, 16, 20, 41, 94, 119; abets France vis-à-vis Czechoslovakia, 13
Bulgaria, 115

Cambodia, 117
Canada, 6
Carlsbad Programme, 21
Carthaginian Peace, 16
Casimir the Great, 43
CENTO (Central Treaty Organization), 79

Ceylon, 5
Chamberlain, Neville, 16, 18, 20, 22, 23, 39, 41 and n., 42 and n., 43, 46, 119
China, 6, 9, 85, 117, 121
Christianity, 64
Churchill, Sir Winston, 99
Class A, class B, and class C powers, 5
Continuation War (Finland v. USSR, 1941–4), 104, 127
Cuba, 77
Czechoslovakia, 7, 10, 13 ff., 81, 97, 102, 103, 118 ff., 127; 'a model small state', 14; population in 1938, 14; minority populations, 14; military alliances, 14; produce, industries, education, and defence, 14–15; Skoda armaments works, 15; cost of surrender to Germany, 15; military implications, 15; collapse under combined pressure from powers, 16; German intentions towards, 16–17; basis of Czech foreign policy, 17; Czechoslovak Legions, 17, 27; Masaryk and Beneš, 17; nationhood, 17; 'the spear in the side of Germany', 18; German offer of non-aggression pact, 18 and nn.; political loyalty to France, 19; faith in French alliance, 19 and n.; as keystone of the Versailles arch, 20; 'ready to honour treaties in all circumstances', 20; concessions to Germany proposed by the West, 21; Lord Runciman accepted as 'Mediator', 21; Carlsbad Programme, 21; makes two vital concessions, 22; army opposes surrender, 22 n.; Franco-Czech Alliance collapses, 24; guarantees offered by Western powers, 24; state of Czech forces in 1938, 26 ff.; pre-Munich frontiers, 28; German forces available for attack on, 28 ff.; Czech strategic advantages, 29; Hitler's plan of battle, 29 f.; Czech generals' confidence that German attack could be withstood, 32; General Syrový's broadcast, 35; French decision to dissociate from, 37; consultations with Russians, 38; Sudeten German invasion, 39; capitulation to Anglo-